WHERE IN THE WORLD?

TRAVELS AND TRAVAILS IN SEARCH OF THE GOOD LIFE

WHERE IN THE WORLD?

TRAVELS AND TRAVAILS IN SEARCH OF THE GOOD LIFE

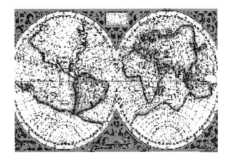

TONY DEL PRETE

Cathedral Publishing
Pittsburgh, PA 15260

Cathedral Publishing
Pittsburgh, PA 15260
(412) 624-6135

Manufactured in the
United States of America

Printed on acid-free paper

ISBN 1-887969-02-0

This book is for my wife, travel companion and best friend, Cyd, who helped make this trip, this book, this life possible.

LAURIE & FRANK

WONDER, THEN WANDER.
BEST OF LIFE AND LUCK.

Ray Del Rex

ACKNOWLEDGMENTS

There are many people I would like to thank for making this book possible, because my family, friends and supporters encouraged me both to take the trip *and* write the book.

Thanks to my Dad and Joyce for keeping track of our finances and mail while we were gone; Holly and Larry for checking in on Cyd's house; and various other family members for their best wishes and contributions to our trip fund. It was also a relief to know that my sister, Alisa, was maintaining our only car and my brother, Al, was keeping everyone abreast of world politics particular to our itinerary. Our good friends Constance and Beth chipped in by taking good care of Burt the cat.

I would also like to thank Frank Lehner and Megan Davidson, whose guidance and editorial comments helped make this book come to life. Cathy Johnson, Rege Behe and Steve Babych provided input and insights on the early drafts. And Ric Anthony and Bill Proudfoot could never know how much their influence, experience and expertise contributed to my writing this book, and writing it well.

I would be remiss if I didn't thank three of the most influential people in my academic past, Judy Vollmer, Donald Reilly and Guy Rossetti, without whose tutelage and encouragement I would not have pursued writing as a vocation upon graduating.

In closing, I wish to thank everyone who, as a large group of supporters, some wishing they too were on the trip, kept us in their thoughts and hearts while we were gone.

TABLE OF CONTENTS

PROLOGUE

As I young boy, I used to spend hours with my brother and sister playing a game we called "Where in the World?" It entailed closing our eyes and spinning the globe to predict what life had in store for us. I can still recall the feeling of the globe's smooth steel surface slipping under my finger as I pressed lightly down on it. When the globe finally came to a halt, I'd shout "This is where I'll get married" or "This is where I'll work," then I'd open my eyes and try to pronounce countries such as Kamchatka and Bophuthatswana.

Later, while growing up, I would marvel at *National Geographic* magazines or watch "Mutual of Omaha's Wild Kingdom," envying Jim Fowler as he wrestled anacondas, Marlin Perkins looking on from the safety of a boat. In grade school, I remember coloring a room-sized mural of Africa, and trying to say Tegucigalpa without my front "teef." I also recall the first time I'd heard the population of China would soon eclipse one billion people.

During my teens and early twenties, I hitch-hiked, drove and jetted across much of the United States, Canada and the Caribbean. But it was all too soon before I began working. Then, like many people, I spent most of my two weeks' vacation visiting relatives. Somehow that wasn't enough, but I didn't know what else to do.

It was in the late 1980s when I noticed in the news and on television that people were beginning to re-examine the quality of their lives. Reports of Wall Street executives moving to Montana, Japanese hippies dropping out and British teens living in bus caravans gave me hope that I could find the simple life too.

Then, in a curious twist of fate, I met Cyd. She had traveled the US and Europe and we would often recount our travels when we got together. It was during one of our early discussions that we decided to go around the world, literally. We would take a calculated risk and see how the rest of the world lived, knowing that one day we would return home, more enlightened and alive than before we left.

XI

At the time, we were two ordinary people with everyday jobs. We weren't rich, but we lived comfortably. Most people would have been satisfied with their lives and overwhelmed by the prospect of giving up so much. Yet, in that moment, we chose to break out of our typical lives. From the minute we made our decision to leave the good life in search of unknown adventure and discovery, there was no turning back.

I'm not sure how Cyd felt at the time, but I was transformed into that little boy again. My heart raced and my mind whirled at the thought of visiting places that until now were only a figment of my childhood imagination. I would have an opportunity once again to play "Where in the World?", only this time the globe, the exotic countries and the itinerary were real.

The dream that I realized and then captured in this book is not for everyone, but the simple philosophy behind it is. To me, you get one chance to make the most of your existence on this planet. And in the long run, whether it's making time to travel, change careers, continue education or take up a hobby, you really don't have to answer to anyone but yourself. Simply put the first domino in motion, the rest will fall into place.

WHERE IN THE WORLD?

TRAVELS AND TRAVAILS IN
SEARCH OF THE GOOD LIFE

CHAPTER 1 ———————————

ONCE UPON A TRIP

I've always believed that people, ordinary everyday people, even fictional people in the literary classics, spend their lives wandering the world in search of answers. Don Quixote tilted at windmills. Santiago rowed out too far. Dante descended to the depths of Hell. Each explorer was, in his own way, looking for challenges and truths that he could not find in the struggle of daily living.

Each traveler also had a partner or companion to explore the land, sea and heavens, or hell, as the case may be. Someone to help him understand the strange or inexplicable. Someone to share the wonder, glory and joy of discovery. Someone to remember the lessons learned when it was all said and done.

And so it was when my new girlfriend, Cyd, and I decided to quit our jobs, put our lives in storage and circle the globe in search of answers. Much like Jules Verne's famous duo, Phileas Fogg and his ever-trusting Passepartout, we were sure of only one thing, that our starting point would also be our final destination. What could or would happen along the way was anyone's guess.

The idea of a world sojourn was spawned during a weekend trip to Lake Erie, but in retrospect I think the seed was planted a long time before that. The decision was made in a matter of seconds when Cyd asked, "Wouldn't it be great if we could see all the beaches of the world?" and I replied, "Why not?" Our minds whirled with excitement at the prospect of not working, not worrying about mortgage or car payments, not answering phones or sitting in traffic jams. We had the opportunity to do what everyone always threatens to do, quit our jobs and experience a life of no worries. And we were going to do it.

The days, weeks, months and, eventually, year that followed our enlightenment entailed hours of reading and research and preparation for putting the brakes on our hectic lives and stepping out of the rat race for awhile. We busied ourselves with hundreds of tasks while juggling the day-to-day regimen of living. Work, friends, family and just about everything else became secondary to the trip; even our newly formed relationship was frozen, a cryogenic affair that would be thawed upon completion of our journey.

Sure we had our doubts, and doubters, but once we made up our minds we knew it was going to happen. I drew a tentative itinerary on the giant map now covering my bedroom wall, as well as a duplicate copy hanging over Cyd's kitchen sink. A black line arched across the Atlantic Ocean, ending at a smudged dot that represented our first stop in London. Subsequent arcs found targets in Hong Kong, Singapore, Bali, Sydney, Auckland and Hawaii, before landing again stateside. I awoke every morning for the next year to the dream of a lifetime penciled on that map.

Our detractors were few and relatively passive, although I couldn't blame anyone for wondering why Cyd was going around the world with a guy she knew less than six months. Occasionally someone would question our sanity for "giving up good paying jobs" or visiting "unsafe, uncivilized places." One person even claimed we would be eaten by cannibals in Borneo. Of course, he was joking, but we had had enough of the good old US-of-A and wanted to see how the rest of the world lived, knowing full well that we could return any time we had the urge.

Once we decided to chuck our stable and easy-going lifestyles, Cyd and I began planning our escape by reading *Time Out* by Bonnie Rubin, which provided us with helpful hints and insights for leaving good-paying jobs, our families and friends, as well as how to re-enter the States refreshed and with an enlightened attitude. That was for us. Satisfied that we could pull it off, we first delineated hunting and gathering information: Cyd was responsible for her points of interest (Indonesia and New Zealand) and I took Southeast Asia, Australia and everything else. Once we decided on a general itinerary, taking into account weather and tourist season and other factors along the way,

2

we researched airline tickets and bus passes, visas and discounts, and various other money-saving devices for the extended stay abroad.

We read numerous other books, such as Bruce Chatwin's *The Songlines* and *The Painted Alphabet* by Diana Darling, to name a few, to get a flavor of the cultures and countries we'd be visiting. I also studied Mandarin Chinese and Indonesian (which was rather easy, and useful in Malaysia as well) to help bridge any communication gaps and hopefully gain the trust of locals, as well as locate the toilets when nature called.

Next we purchased *Southeast Asia on a Shoestring* and its sister guidebook for Australia (which are distributed by Lonely Planet Publications), both invaluable sources of places to go, stay and eat while traveling in foreign lands. We sent for information from embassies and consulates, and kept a close eye on foreign affairs in the event of political unrest. Maps were also a key part of our planning.

We talked with people who had visited sites along our proposed route and contacted friends, relatives and friends-of-friends living abroad who might be willing to put us up and show us around. (As it turned out, the people we stayed with were happy to see familiar faces and receive word from home.)

The months before we were due to leave were filled with last-minute job obligations and money matters. (In fact, Cyd and I helped find replacements for our vacant positions.) We found various ways to save or raise money, like the yard sale which netted us $300 and the last-minute sale of my car which brought in another $2,000. We also received gifts and donations from family, friends and co-workers (I'll never forget the going-away party and $153.48 my work colleagues gave us for the trip). Everyone was glad, albeit a bit envious, that we were doing what they always wanted to do.

We visited the dentist and doctor to head off any unforeseen medical problems, as well as the public health department to obtain necessary shots and inoculations. As a precaution, we also continued our insurance plans with our employers and kept our car insurance active so as not to increase our rates upon return. We found renters to house-sit Cyd's place in our absence and friends who would watch her cat. I worked a deal with my landlord to pay the last month's rent with my security deposit. We left no stone unturned in our quest for cash and raised most of the money we needed for the trip in a little less than a year's time.

As our departure date drew nearer, time sped up like a race car's revving engine ready to take off at the drop of the flag. The thought of leaving our family and friends and all the comforts of home became evident the day we purchased our one-way tickets around the world. After literally signing our lives away, Cyd jumped up and, in a frenzy of happiness, smashed our mouths together in a reckless kiss of chipped teeth and split lips.

The morning of our departure we tied up some loose ends. All we had left was to cram our backpacks with everything and anything we'd need for six months on the road. Of course, packing everything we'd need turned out to be a highly interpretive and uniquely gender-specific concept, but we managed. We planned for hot and cold weather, opting for comfort and clothes that could be applied and removed in layers. We also allowed for wet and dry climates, stuffing hats, rain gear and aqua-socks into pockets of our backpacks.

But it was too late now to worry about our bags as we hurried to the Pittsburgh International Airport. Soon, the engine of our commuter flight to Washington, DC warmed up on the runway, 100 pounds of our belongings in its belly. Once in our seats, we held hands across the narrow aisle and contemplated where this trip would eventually take us, not knowing for certain whether we would be the same when we returned. We closed our eyes and took a collective deep breath in anticipation of what the upcoming months would gift us with and secretly thanked God for the chance to realize what for most people remains only a dream.

The jet rose from the runway in a sweeping curve that represented the first arc on our giant maps, which were now folded and packed away with the rest of our belongings not to be seen again until the next year. We broke free of the cloud cover that is typical of springtime in Pennsylvania and welcomed warm sunshine and thoughts of distant, unknown beaches.

LONDON FOG

I had heard that Atlantic crossings can have a way of taking the air out of your balloon, especially when you can't sleep on an overnight flight, and this trip was no exception. We descended through dreary gray clouds that reminded us of home and landed at Heathrow International Airport just after breakfast. Still in a fog from the flight, we stood in line at the customs gate, juggling our day packs and valuables as nationals from around the world paraded by with tan and black and blood-red passports. After gaining entry to England, we called our friend, Lisa, who had offered to put us up for the week, and wearily sought the London Underground, or Tube as it's commonly known.

Queasy and exhausted from the weeks of preparation and lack of sleep, I coaxed Cyd along while hauling the two backpacks for what seemed like miles toward the Tube. Once seated on the train, I began to wonder if it was all worth it and whether we could handle months of this type of travel. I wasn't doubting the trip, just the energy required to endure it. But as the train rose up out of the ground and trundled past rows of simple ivy-clad buildings with crisscrossing antennas outlined against the foggy sky, my heart raced at the thought of our first discovery, England.

I looked over at Cyd, her head bobbing as she tried to fight off sleep. Her dark hair had grown out in the weeks leading up to our departure, its curls now covering her face like a veil. Breathing deeply, she looked at peace.

"We're almost there," I whispered in a raspy voice.

Cyd opened her eyes and smiled at me. She seemed to summon all of her strength to say, "Happy birthday." Then she drifted back to sleep.

5

With all the last-minute activities and excitement of leaving, I had actually forgotten it was my birthday. I was thirty-three, an age when Christ claimed a man should know what it is he wanted to do with his life. I had never really been sure of what I wanted to do with my life. I did know what I *didn't* want to do, and that was live to work. I thought maybe somehow this trip would help me determine the direction of my future.

At the Hampstead station we took the elevator to street level and got our first peek at London. Quaint cafes and two-story Brownstones dominated the narrow street, with pubs and pharmacies and small businesses squeezed in between as an afterthought. People clad in spring wools and sweaters scurried to work in the fine mist of the early morning. Sleek, compact cars and motorcycles zoomed by as pedestrians darted in and out of traffic.

As I took in a deep breath I realized we were no longer part of the 9-to-5 crowd. We could eat and sleep when we wanted to, unencumbered by time constraints or obligations to family, friends and employers. The calendar as we knew it, Sunday to Monday, June to December, 1991 to 1992, no longer existed except for plane and bus schedules and what time the cafes closed. Much in the same manner as an earthquake rerouting a river, our course in life had been changed forever, never to be the same again.

Lisa sat under a newsstand next to the Underground exit, eating a pastry and reading the morning paper. An American to the core, she was oblivious to the bustle of the street and our presence. I gently nudged her leg. With a wry smile and bear hug she welcomed us to Hampstead. "You two look like zombies," Lisa said dryly as she shouldered one of our bags. "You can have my bed for the week."

After a long nap we whiled away our first day in London by taking a leisurely stroll through the market at Camden. The dark broth of the canal and black attire of street urchins did not dampen the atmosphere as mimes and jugglers and musicians performed for their suppers.

In the week ahead Lisa showed us both sides of the city: first accompanying us on a double-decker bus tour, and then planning a picnic near Karl Marx's tombstone in Highgate Cemetery. Postcards came to life as we walked or bused past Big Ben and Buckingham Palace, the Thames and Tower Bridge. We drank ales at the Punch and Judy Pub, overlooking street players at Covent Garden and basking in the uncharacteristically bright sunshine of London. I talked cricket with a man in Piccadilly Circus and watched Wimbledon at a pub in Brighton Beach.

The Fourth of July came and went without a snap, crackle or pop. No fireworks. No barbecues. No parades. Yet Cyd and I were celebrating our own very different kind of independence. Like snakes, we had shed our collective skins and wriggled with the prospect of a new life, our senses heightened, the excess baggage removed. We were changing (into what we weren't sure), but once the process had begun, there was no turning back.

One night when Lisa was working we wandered down to the Thames River, coming to rest at Cleopatra's Needle, a towering jet-black obelisk that had weathered prior regimes and war and had the pock marks from bomb shrapnel to prove it. From there we followed the flow of the Thames and soon found ourselves in need of a rest room. I approached a kind looking porter and asked if he knew where a rest room was.

"Rest room," he chuckled. "Why do you Americans insist on calling it a rest room? Are you tired?" He laughed again displaying a mouthful of piano ivories. "We Brits call it a toilet."

"But toilet is such a vulgar word," I replied.

He politely pointed back in the direction we came. "The 'toilet' is just there on the left, gov'na." An echo of laughter followed in our footsteps as we hurried off.

Upon our return to the riverside, the porter beckoned us again. More English lessons, I thought. But to our surprise, he leaned close and told us of a scheduled ghost tour through lower London that would be starting shortly. He winked and bid us "Ta," when we heard the polite voice of the guide call for attention. We moved in the direction

7

of a small group huddled around a man who we guessed was the tour guide. I turned back to thank the porter and he was gone.

The tour guide introduced himself as Graham. He was a portly middle-age gent with gray hair and a blue-red nose, stubby fingers and bulldog jowls that brought to mind a character in a Dickens's novel. As he provided an overview of the tour, dressed in a drab jacket and cardigan, I guessed that he read a lot and frequented the pub even more.

He led our group through London proper, this pied piper of the paranormal, whispering tales of murder and hauntings as he pointed to windows and alleyways that were the stage of occasional ghost sightings. In addition to numerous haunted hideaways the tour offered, Graham shared his nostalgia for Buckingham Palace and revealed the touching inscription of "Faith, hope and love" at the base of Alexandria's Statue.

As Graham recounted a gruesome story about the murder of one man's mistress and her haunting ways, I found myself thinking about what people were doing back home. I wondered what life would be like for people without me and Cyd in their lives. I hoped selfishly that our absence might make things somehow less exciting or novel for others, but in my heart I knew that our leaving wouldn't really make a difference. In a way I knew what it was like to die and have only your memory live on in the minds of people who remembered you. It wasn't a comforting feeling.

The tour ended and, bearing out my initial impressions of Graham, he suggested we sample a few pints at Porter's Pub, a rustic little ale house built in the early 1500s. Later, as we parted company, walking the cobblestone lane beneath the gas street lamps, Cyd and I huddled for warmth in the night's cool, damp air. "We're doing the right thing, aren't we?" Cyd asked. "There's no doubt in my mind," I said. For the rest of our walk home we said nothing.

POISON IVY IN ELLESMERE PORT?

I hadn't seen my cousin Gary in almost 30 years. In fact, he was raised in San Francisco and I'd only met him once at the age of three. He was now living in northern England and had graciously offered to put us up for a while. Prior to our trip I had mailed him an outdated photo of me and called from London to tell him our train schedule. I was sure we would have a wonderful reunion. But shortly after our arrival in the sleepy canal town of Ellesmere Port, Gary and his wife, Angeline, were driving me to the Duchess's Hospital to seek treatment for poison ivy, which I had contracted only days before our departure. It had gotten worse in the days since we left, so I had no recourse but to seek help.

Once inside the hospital, I explained my case to the befuddled clerk as I filled out a few forms. She had never heard of "poison ivory," or whatever I had called it, and admitted me immediately. The orderly whisked me by coughing and sickly children and injured adults, concerned that I might contaminate all of England if not treated right away. I thought about sneaking out the back door to avoid further embarrassment, but the prospect of having poison ivy upon arriving in Hong Kong's triple-digit heat and humidity kept me on the gurney.

A female doctor in her early thirties soon appeared, medical dictionary in hand. After explaining that she had never seen poison ivy (which does not exist in England), she asked if we could show other doctors and interns what it looked like before we treated it. I felt like a freak in a sideshow, but I wanted to be treated, so I consented.

During the doctor's examination I discussed several treatments I knew of for poison ivy with the curious group of interns. They thanked me for my cooperation and, filled with knowledge they might never use, went on their way. The attending physician prescribed a steroid cream and sent me to the on-site pharmacy to have it filled. England's national health plan footed the bill, which cost only eight dollars (including parking) and a piece of humble pie on the ride home.

Now that I was healthy, we began touring the area. The days that followed took us to Liverpool and Cavern Street where the Beatles hatched their careers. While Gary and Angie worked, Cyd and I meandered around the streets of Ellesmere, admiring the many manicured gardens that seemed to overwhelm every yard and exploring the canals that at one time made Ellesmere a very busy port.

On our last night in Ellesmere, our gracious hosts took us on a sunset drive through misty Birkenhead and the Wirral. Walking along a stone wall near the road, we looked out over the Parkgate marshes that stretch longingly toward the hazy blue Cambrian Mountains of Wales. This was far away from London in style and natural grandeur and I could now understand why Angie never felt a need to leave. And for the first time, I missed being home. I missed my family and friends, Tuesday night basketball with the guys, the people at work. Strangely, though, I didn't miss much of anything else. The phone calls, bills, driving a car all seemed so foreign to me now.

Later, as the sun set, we dined at the Tudor Rose, a traditional English pub. After a few pints of Strongbow, I sampled a crock of the infamous steak and kidney pie. It wasn't too bad for English fare, considering that the British favor beans and toast for breakfast. During dinner Angie suggested before we return to London that we visit the walled city of Chester, which was only a short way down the railway from Ellesmere Port. It would cost us a few extra *quid* to change our rail tickets, but she insisted it would be worth our while.

With little debate we decided to go. (Prior to departing on the trip, Cyd and I had discussed finances in great length. We had saved for one year and parlayed that money with some savings which would allow us to live on approximately sixty dollars a day. That included food, transportation [other than plane fare], lodging and the mundane costs of living, such as washing clothes and buying newspapers. In addition, we had agreed to take advantage of any once-in-a-lifetime opportunities; we could pay for overruns when we got back home.)

When we first came up out of the rail station, Chester looked like any other European town. Quiet narrow streets are filled with animated pedestrians on their way to market. Short, squat buildings give way to church spires and steeples, which spike the low hanging clouds and fog. Signs and chalkboards and window dressings purport the day's fare. Yet, as we walked the great stone wall encompassing the city limits, we were transported back to a time when cafes sported only six-foot high ceilings and horse-drawn carriages bounced along the cobblestones. It was dizzying to think that places like the Blue Bell restaurant have been a part of Chester since Columbus first set sail for America.

Chester stands as a reminder of the western expanse of the Roman Empire; when you're marching it's a long way from Italy. The encircling wall was originally built in 79 AD for protective purposes and in the millennia since, turrets and passageways have been added by reigning monarchs and dukes alike. The cathedral and square date back to the 13th century and, thanks to the reconstruction efforts of Saint Anselm, have endured changing times and unyielding weather.

We circled the entire city in search of the Bridge of Sighs, only to catch a quick glimpse of it as our bus departed through the north gate. The relaxing pace inside the walls and along the outer canals was the perfect nightcap for our visit to England. The first leg of our trip was complete; it was time to go. We caught the train back to London for some quick good-byes and thank yous, then a final ride on the Tube to Heathrow Airport.

SALAD STACKING IN SHATIN, AND OTHER ORIENTAL MYSTERIES

The overnight flight for Hong Kong departed in a fine afternoon drizzle that is synonymous with London. Before long the first wave of darkness obscured the blurry landscape below, and we turned our attention to filling the 14-hour trip with things to do. Cyd raided the magazine rack while I busied myself reading up on Hong Kong and other sites we might explore. After several tasty meals, including poached salmon and steak filets, we stretched out across a center row of seats (which Cyd had negotiated when we booked our flight) and took turns napping while "Dances with Wolves" flashed on the bulkhead's giant movie screen. It was the first of many US films we would see during the months ahead, which provided us with a comforting but sometimes bothersome reminder of home.

In the early hours before dawn, with most of the passengers somewhere between sleep and their destination, I awoke to the gleeful thought of replacing work with travel for as long as our money held out. As I drifted back to sleep, thoughts of simple, easy living danced in my head. The next time I opened my eyes we were descending into the first orange glow of dawn, which cast blinding rays of sunlight off the glassy skyscrapers of Hong Kong city.

Pushing our way through the cattle call at customs, we eventually met up with another friend, Christie (with her infant son, Jesse), who had come to chaperon us back to their apartment in Hong Kong's mid level. The four of us caught the Star Ferry to the island of Hong Kong, where 5 million people push and shove and spit and holler all day long. In fact, I felt right at home when I conducted a ritual that I had done all my life by spitting in the water. I don't know why, but it makes me feel as if I'm part of the body of water and forever a part of the place I visit.

Though covered with a film of oil and industrial flotsam, the water of the harbor caught the sun's rays and threw them upward in a mix of turquoise and white hot sparkles. I closed my eyes and turned my face upward to bask in the sun and my newfound freedom, while Cyd and Christie caught each other up on their lives.

Once on the island, we joined the queue for a taxi among natty Chinese businessmen and disheveled laborers who stood waiting rigidly without comment. We jumped into a red and white cab and Christie instructed the driver where to go. "*Num bah two, say mo do,*" Christie said in a sing-song cadence to the driver, who nodded and tripped the meter. "That's how you tell them our address,"

Christie explained. "Number two, Seymour Road." It was nothing like the Mandarin I had studied.

Pulling up in front of the drab building that would be our home for a while, I thought about what brought us to Hong Kong and the Orient: the ancient cultures, unexplored countryside, communism, our ex-patriot friends Bill and Christie. (We had thought it would be a much easier transition if we could visit with some English-speaking friends on our first stop so far from home.)

Christie, Bill and baby Jesse, had just moved from a tiny apartment on the outskirts of Kowloon to a large art-deco studio in Hong Kong's affluent mid level. Our arrival coincided with their move, so we lent a hand while catching up on our lives. Pangs of homesickness came and went as we all reminisced amid boxes scattered around the apartment.

Bill was also busy with work, so Christie offered to be our guide for the next few weeks. During that time we saw The Temple of 10,000 Buddhas (which was more like the Temple of 10,000 Steps), Tiger Balm Garders, the mid-level zoo and botanical gardens. We sampled international cuisine and authentic Chinese food. In addition, we may have witnessed the strangest custom known to man, an act I later labeled "salad stacking."

En route from Hong Kong to Fanling, a backward village in the New Territories that abuts bordering mountains of China, we stopped in Shatin. Longing for home cooking or anything that smacked of the United States, we ate lunch at a Pizza Hut. Some unknown countryside, I thought.

The pizza understandably left a lot to be desired, tasting more like barbecue sauce on bread, but the show the Chinese put on at the salad bar was better than any rite or ritual we saw while in Southeast Asia. First, each patron carefully built a foundation of cucumbers and olives to fill the bottom of the wooden bowl. Then, they meticulously chose leaves of lettuce, about the size of credit cards, so as not to take up too much space. This layer was covered with a coating of cheese, then pickles, onions and carrot slices, all weighed and measured to fit within the blueprint. By culinary standards the bowl was filled, but the architectural genius of generations past was about to unfold in the form of the ultimate salad monument. Another ring of cucumbers extended the bowl by exactly one-half a slice, and the process of filling and stacking began anew. The result was an inverted 10-inch cone of salad that could have, and did, feed a family of four, as we witnessed when one person brought the salad back to the table. Having had our fill of Chinese culture and curiosity, we boarded the train and returned home. Leery of the Confucian saying that 'One should be careful of what one wishes for, it might come true,' I hoped that our boat trip to China the next day would be as unique and exciting as this day was.

That night we sampled plum wine and saki in the penthouse of an 80-story apartment building overlooking Hong Kong harbor. Below, the speeding cars, giant neon billboards and a canyon of skyscrapers reminded me of futuristic Tokyo in the movie "Bladerunner." However, it was the shrieking winds and heavy clouds racing over the mainland that were a portent of what was to come our way. People all over the city where were talking about Typhoon Brendan, a storm worthy of a powerful No. 8 rating, which was on its way to Hong Kong. No one could say for sure what a typhoon might do, and reports were that monsoons had already flooded most of southern China. Cyd and I couldn't help but think that our riverboat tour and down-payment with the travel agency was literally being washed out to sea, an early casualty of Typhoon Brendan.

We awoke the next morning to sheeting rain and hundred mile-per-hour winds that had pushed against the building all night. Well aware of our cancellation fee, Cyd and I put on rain gear and began our descent to the tour's predetermined meeting place in Hong Kong's business district. We never would have done this back home, but this was the Orient, where people take this kind of thing in stride.

Our route was littered with more debris than we had become accustomed to during our walks around Hong

Kong. Windows had been blown out, metal sheeting torn from rooftops. Signposts wavered and stop lights flickered intermittently as the wind buffeted our path. Not a sign of life, not even the chicken man who sang his sad song every morning under the weight of a yoke from which freshly slaughtered chickens hung. I now better understood where the Chinese got the term *Gweilo*, meaning "crazy white devil," but we had paid for the trip and nothing could turn us back, not even a full-blown typhoon.

Drenched and somewhat disheartened, we finally made it to the lobby of the Furama Hotel and waited almost an hour before we threw in the towel and ordered some breakfast. I tried to console Cyd (and convince myself) by explaining that the agency would certainly understand the situation and refund all of our money. Besides, the guide never showed; not until our breakfast came, that is.

In spastic, broken English our sopping wet guide explained our options. "You still go to China," he said emphatically. "By train. We go now."

I dropped my toast. "Right now?" I asked. I looked to Cyd for a response. Before leaving on the trip I had promised Cyd's father I would take care of her. Recalling his flippant threat of hunting me down with a shotgun if anything happened, I declined our guide's offer with a dismissing wave.

"It safe," the guide replied. "You go?" Water dripped from the hair plastered to his forehead. He mindlessly wiped the steam off his glasses using a wet shirt tail and rhetorically asked again: "You go?"

For the first time I said no and meant it. I tried to explain that it was dangerous, but he had gotten the message and was gone, I presumed to gather up whoever was still waiting in the typhoon. I couldn't imagine anyone wanting so badly to go to China that they would risk their lives but, after all, it did cost $250 per person, which was almost two weeks of our budget. Still soaking wet, we finished eating and hailed an ice-cold cab back to the apartment. Before we went to sleep, we tentatively planned our strategy for dealing with the agency when the storm let up.

It was after noon when we awoke for the second time that day. The typhoon had subsided, but now we had to prepare ourselves for a force greater than nature: getting a refund from a Chinese travel agency. Before we left for the agency, I called Visa to explain what had happened and they were very supportive. If nothing else, we knew we could contest the charge upon our return stateside, but that wouldn't be for months.

There still weren't many people on the streets as we approached China Travel. Once inside we adopted forlorned looks and innocently questioned the clerk about our problem. We tried to explain our misfortune, adopting various styles of negotiation to get through to the clerk. His poker face made it difficult to determine how things were going, so we took a more direct approach, demanding our money back. "Solly," he deadpanned. "It the lules." He pointed to the disclaimer on our tickets that indicated only partial refund in the event of a natural disaster. Not a bad business practice, I thought, in a part of the world where this type of thing occurs frequently.

Cyd tried a more accommodating approach, explaining that we were budget travelers and had to recover our money in order to make it through the next few months of the trip. Again, but this time with a smile, he declined. "Only part refund," he said. With that I realized that he was "just doing his job," and we would have to go over his head to get satisfaction. It appeared that East and West were not that far apart after all.

The manager, a large, menacing woman who spoke softly, almost apologetically, was summoned and, after placing a follow-up call to our guide, offered us a 50 percent refund. With a smile she stated that the refund could be applied to another tour.

Yeah, that's just what we wanted to do, I thought. Reinvest what's left of our money in a three-day tour of the now flooded, typhoon-racked streets of Guangzhou, sidestepping hepatitis and typhoid as we slogged to tourist destinations in the hills. "No thanks," I said flatly.

It was then that Cyd began to cry. Partly out of frustration and loss, and partly as a ploy in a last-ditch effort to reclaim a full refund. I also thought she might be homesick.

In typical Chinese fashion, the manager never blinked. So much for the customer always being right, I thought. Yet as disappointed and angry as we were, we later had to laugh at how it all made sense to her. After all, storms and typhoons come and go in this part of the world. People die. Flood waters rise and fall. And no matter what the occasion, no matter how dangerous the situation might appear to us, this woman, along with the other 5 million inhabitants of the island, board the endless stream of buses and trolleys and cabs each day to go to work. Even when there's a typhoon.

Somewhat stunned but undaunted, we now had a few extra days on our hands and decided to visit Macao, another island in the gulf, which was once a stopover for Portuguese galleons, pirates and seafaring traders. The country is actually made up of the city of Macao and two tiny islands, Taipa and Coloane, which are linked by a bridge and causeway respectively.

We left the city early the next morning by hydrofoil, zooming across the blue-brown waters of Zhujiang Kou bay to our destination 30 miles southwest of Hong Kong. After a quick spin through customs, we made for the rental car company, Macao Mokes, and selected a *moke*. Our vehicle for the day resembled a golf cart, army green with a white leather convertible roof and off-road tires. It had no doors, sparse interior and the steering wheel on the right-hand side. Perfect for Macao.

In my excitement, I jumped in and started her up. The engine came to life with a sputter, reminding me of my lawn mower (which I no longer owned) after a winter hibernation. But that wouldn't dampen our spirits on this bright, sunny Macao day. I put the moke in gear and turned out onto the single roadway that encircles this island city rich in Portuguese history and Chinese culture.

Cars swerved and weaved on all sides of the moke as I attempted to navigate through traffic that rivaled the upcoming Grand Prix. Horns blared, exhaust fumes burned our throats and noses. It had only taken several hundred yards for the novelty to wear off. We were going 40 miles per hour amid madcap Macao motorists, when I turned to Cyd and said, "You know, I haven't driven a stick in a long time." Our eyes met in mutual panic as the bridge to Taipa loomed ahead.

Now it's true that driving a stick is like riding a bike, but it's also important to remember that practice makes perfect, too. Throw in left-side driving, unfamiliar streets and shifting with your left hand, and standard shift takes on a whole new meaning.

Without event I managed to veer across several lanes and pull into a parking space that overlooked the bay. Cyd was laughing too hard to be upset and offered to take the wheel. We regained our composure, checked our map and set sights for the inner city. All systems were go, except that Cyd couldn't back out of the space. We tried everything possible to position the shifter in reverse, but to no avail. To the delight of tourists and nationals alike, I would be our "reverse" for the day. After a brief lull in the traffic, I pushed the moke out onto the roadway and we were off.

The road was lined with churches and temples, juxtaposing western and oriental religions in a surreal cityscape. We discovered that the people of Macao are predominately Chinese, but there is a large Portuguese population, as well as numerous other immigrants. After a somewhat harrowing drive around the perimeter of the city, dodging parked trucks spewing noxious fumes and pedestrians and mopeds zigzagging in every direction, we opted for the more sedate setting of the outer islands.

Once across the bridge to Taipa we entered another world, where the litter and concrete of Macao was transformed into flowers and verdant foliage. We puttered along the narrow two-lane road, occasionally stopping at villages where I would practice my Chinese and the villagers would try their English. Their warm, shy smiles would invite photos, but we were often politely waved off. It was that way throughout our visit to Southeast Asia, where people going about their everyday lives didn't want to be part of our memoirs, and we could understand that.

18

Heck, if somebody strolled up to my house and started taking pictures, I'd probably have something to say about it, too.

On a friend's recommendation we decided to try a little tavern on Taipa called Pinocchio's, reputed to have huge prawns and good wine. After traversing side streets and alleyways, I finally put my ego aside and hopped out of the moke to ask directions. I approached a watchman at what appeared to be a deserted race track or casino and bid him hello. "*Ni hao*," I offered with a wave.

He stared blankly at me and shrugged.

Stumped for a moment, I took a new tack. "*Hablas Espanol?*" I asked hopefully.

His eyes popped wide as he shouted *Si, senor!*" and offered his weathered hand.

In a mishmash of Spanish, English and Portuguese I translated the directions to the tavern.

"*Rua do Sol*," the watchman chirped proudly.

With an "*Adios, amigo*" we were on our way again.

Lunch at Pinocchio's was a success as we sampled huge shrimp in sauce and got a taste of Taipa's culture all in one sitting. Portuguese children scampered under and around the tables much to the disdain of the watchful Chinese elders. The spacious room filled with shouts in Portuguese and Chinese and Malay and Thai that blended in a cultural cacophony while we whispered hopes that the development on nearby Macao wouldn't find its way to this island, and that these people could continue to live like this forever.

After lunch we crossed the mile-long causeway between Taipa and Coloane, the stench from dried tidal flats and a nearby dump permeating the heavy, humid air for the entire stretch of road. There isn't much to see or do on Coloane, but we did find Hac Sa Beach, a stony inlet which provided a disconcerting view of strip-mining activities on the opposite hillside. We stayed for a short while and returned to our trusty moke, which to our surprise, was now covered with a large sack cloth tied to adjacent palm trees. As we curiously approached the moke, an old Chinese man with sparse teeth and gnarled hands began to untie the tent-like covering. He bowed respectfully and offered his hands, begging payment for watching over our vehicle and providing shade from the hot afternoon sun. I tossed him a few odd coins and he nodded appreciatively. Then I pushed the moke out of its parking space and looked over my shoulder as he quizzically scratched his head.

Crossing over the stinking causeway and then the bridge to "civilization," I thought about the enterprising old man in the pointed straw hat. I could still see his leathery skin and sullen, hopeful eyes, his tattered clothes in worse shape than the burlap he used for shade. How many mokes had he carefully secured and stood guard over to make enough money for his family to eat rice that night? Again I was reminded how fortunate we were.

Safely back at the rental office, the owner of Macao Mokes, a middle-aged Portuguese man, offered to drive us to the dock and the afternoon hydrofoil. During our ride he lamented the imminent Chinese takeover in 1999, two years after the scheduled change-over for Hong Kong. He quietly explained that people in Macao (and probably Hong Kong, for that matter) lived in ramshackle huts surrounded by barbed wire and concrete walls, not because they feared an invasion, but because they wanted to protect their belongings.

"But why not live in a nice place, too?" Cyd asked.

"You see, when the Chinese come," he continued, "they will tax and take property. So we spend money on things we can take with us. Nice cars. Stereos. Anything we can move out when they come." He proceeded to tell us how the Chinese government promised to pay double, and even triple, the real estate value for established businesses, but that didn't interest him. He said that he was already making plans to move, "Maybe to Australia or Canada."

"Good luck," Cyd said, as our driver deposited us at the ferry terminal. "You'll work something out."

"I'm afraid we don't have any choice," he replied with a grimace. "Macao will be no more." He quickly sped off.

There is much debate as to what the Chinese will do when they take over Hong Kong and Macao, and possibly even Taiwan. It was hard for me to believe that the free-wheeling capitalism that was synonymous with Hong Kong will remain intact. In fact, we learned many companies and organizations were already pulling out or making plans to move to Australia and other nearby countries. It was sad to think that the divergent lifestyles of silk-suited businessmen and burlap-clad villagers could dissolve into one dull, gray appendage of China.

COLLECT CALL FROM BUDDHA

After visiting friends, tasting exotic foods and weathering Typhoon Brendan, we opted to visit Lantau, a rather large, sparsely populated island in the gulf of Hong Kong. Our destination: Po Lin monastery, which is as far away from the steam and smell of Hong Kong as Kansas is from New York.

The ferry arrived at Lantau port just in time for us to catch the No. 6 bus to the youth hostel. The hour-long trip from the pier to the 3,000-foot peak was a pinball ride aboard a rickety school bus which took up most of the lane-and-a-half road snaking its way to Po Lin and our accommodations. The bus bounced and shuttered as we kamikazed up and down scenic ravines, snapping branches off overhanging trees and sending monkeys scurrying for cover. At dusk we skidded to a halt outside the monastery, still shining gold and red in the last light of day. Its ornate spires and molding seemed excessive for monk's accommodations, but who was I to question their one luxury.

We still had a mile trek to the hostel, so we followed the path the driver pointed out and never looked back. We arrived at the hostel in time to grab a quick bite to eat, chat with some other travelers from Britain, Denmark and Canada, chase a giant gecko from our bed and go to sleep. There was only one catch: It had been a week since we talked to anyone stateside, and Cyd wanted to call home. The hostel manager told us that there was a pay phone back at the monastery, so we figured, why not? We had forgotten to bring a flashlight, so I agreed to accompany Cyd along the jungle path. Using only the incandescent light of the moon, we began our trek back to the monastery and, hopefully, the phone.

Seconds after leaving the hostel gate and barbed-wire fences that kept assorted "things" out, the night jungle swallowed us whole. We had become blind to the point that our hearing strained to identify the disquieting, unfamiliar grunts, squeaks and chirps. Each step along the pathway was alive with unknown, invisible and imagined creatures dodging our approach. We talked and whistled nervously as the phantoms grew in size and ferocity just out of harm's way.

As we rounded a bend in the path which we had followed by the feel of gravel underfoot, milky light poured through an opening in the jungle and we quickened our step. Black gave way to blue, then gray as the forest opened into a clearing. Cyd was in front and I heard her gasp as if she'd seen a ghost.

Joining her in the moonlight I stood stunned, as there, perched several hundred feet above us, sitting majestically atop the peak, was a towering, shadowy Buddha backlit only by the full moon and wisps of clouds. After staring in awe for several minutes, we forgot about making that phone call. Instead we wondered, how had we missed the giant icon? Were we still moving at a rapid pace even though we left our jobs more than three weeks ago?

A gentle gulf breeze climbed up through the valley and nudged us back in the direction we came. We quietly retraced our steps to the hostel, unconcerned with the still unfamiliar sounds. Back inside the compound, we crawled onto the plastic mattresses of our bunk beds and drifted off to sleep to the gecko's triumphant clicking as it devoured yet another mosquito.

FROG AND TOAD BARBECUE

One of our first voyages and encounters with capitalism gone awry was on a Sunday outing to Peng Chau, one of the more than 200 tiny islands that neighbor Hong Kong in the gulf. We rejoined our friends Bill and Christie and boarded the inter-island ferry to Cheng Chau, where we debarked. Bill immediately began haggling with a junk owner to charter a trip to Peng Chau. After minutes of loud and animated negotiations, we carefully climbed aboard the dilapidated boat and puttered out to sea. Bill had told us about a gluttonous outdoor barbecue at the Frog and Toad restaurant, and we looked forward to drinking a few beers and pigging out American style.

The pilot of our junk had little trouble navigating the choppy waters between the islands. However, about halfway to Peng Chau, in the middle of the sea, I suddenly heard Bill holler over the growl of the junk's engine: "I knew you were gonna do this, you wanker!" As the gaunt Chinese man smiled and stared out to sea, Bill told me that the owner now wanted more money for taking us across. "They do this all the time," Bill lamented. Then he turned and cursed the smiling man again. Bill and the pilot finally settled on a revised fare, with the difference to be paid upon our return trip.

We hopped off the tiny junk onto a rickety pier with Bill and the pilot still shouting about when he would return and how much it would cost. A narrow boardwalk wound through knee-high grass, concealing clamorous insects and the source of pungent odors that baked in the mid-day sun. In the distance I could see our destination: The Frog and Toad was two stories of civilization rising out of the swamp basin of Peng Chau. As we approached the simple cement structure coated in whitewash, we could hear boisterous Australians (a redundant term if I've ever heard one) shouting and hammering the table, playing a drinking game reminiscent of college parties. The next two hours we dined on barbecued pork and chicken and steak, drinking pitchers of beer and avoiding the sizzling sun. We ate large baked potatoes and corn-on-the-cob and recounted times we all shared back home. Cyd smiled a lot.

The return ride to Cheng Chau was uneventful and our ferry back to Hong Kong pushed through the harbor, which now teemed with giant vessels from around the world. Arab, Russian and African flags flapped listlessly in the intermittent breeze that gave rise to an occasional whitecap on the emerald water. In the distance Hong Kong Island was ringed with a doughnut of clouds, its peak rising above, while skyscrapers of various shapes and sizes seemed to provide support from below. Jesse, only six months old, slept in his stroller. In our brief stay with Bill and Christie he seemed to grow so much, and I couldn't help but wonder how living in this place at such a young age would affect the rest of his life. It certainly had affected mine.

CHAPTER 2 ——————————

SWING SINGAPORE

The next stop on our itinerary was Singapore, which during our travels in Southeast Asia would provide us with a chance to eat safe food, take warm showers, and call home without great difficulty. We operated out of the colorful San Wah Hotel, which was managed by a kindly Chinese gentleman, Chao Yoke San, who schooled me in Mandarin and said I was a "Good Joe."

But as much as Singapore offered us respite from the tiresome and frustrating novelty of traveling in third-world countries, it also reminded us of what can go wrong when governments have too much control. Fines for spitting, not flushing in public toilets, chewing gum, jaywalking and assorted other crimes put up invisible barriers, while gun-toting soldiers at the airport presented a more open reminder that everything was "under control."

In addition to exotic foods and culture, Singapore also presented before us one of the strangest celebrations we'd ever seen. We didn't witness secret rituals or tribal dances or rites of passage, nor fascinating religious ceremonies and age-old customs. Much to our confusion and chagrin, we became part of "Swing Singapore," a gigantic outdoor party sponsored by the government to make the country a more harmonious, and to a great extent homogeneous, place to live. It was a great idea, on rice paper.

In a country the size of Manhattan, with racial and ethnic diversity like nowhere else in the world, where veiled Muslims share the same sidewalk with Thai men in silk suits and Malay women in Emmanuel Lingaro dresses, we found ourselves in the middle of one of the most antiseptic celebrations we'd seen since our high school graduations. Signs everywhere advertised the official drink as bottled water, while people wandered around like multicultural zombies from a George Romero movie. Sophisticated laser lights ricocheted off the many flashy hotels and high-class storefronts, while the sounds of techno-pop echoed down Orchard Road which, by the early evening hours, was filled with as many policemen as pedestrians. We mingled among the thousands of nationals, yet failed to hear even one Chinese firecracker or Indian timpani. Nor did we see a Kabuki dance or Thai procession, only the disco beat of The Manhattan Transfer and incessant cooing from Gerardo, the one-hit Latino wonder.

We would make Singapore our resting spot three times during our six-month trek. In subsequent visits we discovered Little India, China Town and the newly restored Raffles Hotel, as well as numerous alcoves and storefronts rich with Indo-Malay chatter and the click-clack of *mahjongg*. Yet none of these could compare to the otherworldly strangeness of Swing Singapore: a celebration of freedom that was anything but.

BALI HIGHS AND LOWS

A lot has been written over the years about how Bali, the most famous of the 13,000 islands in Indonesia, is becoming too commercial. Sadly, with the influx of resort hotels that cater specifically to the wealthy, we found that to be somewhat true.

However, far from the noisy streets, overpriced shops and crowded beaches of Kuta and Legian, we found the real Bali. There, innocent young girls balanced Coke bottles on their heads as they took turns riding a dilapidated bike around an open field, practicing for the years ahead when they would cart half their weight in rice like that. Young boys embraced their roosters, anticipating the passage of manhood that came with the first cock fight. Timeless elders bathed in creeks and shuffled along the roadside, suspicious of strangers and passersby. We observed and were observed like beings from another planet.

We landed at the airport just before dusk and debarked in the orange afterglow of a Bali sunset. Hundreds of people politely clamored for our attention and offered to take us to Kuta, Legian, or wherever we wanted to go.

Finally we chose Simpang Inn, a spacious square of rooms sequestered away from the main thoroughfare in Legian where a simple room cost $12 a night, including breakfast.

After surveying the room's futon and hardwood closets, sliding across the tiled floor in her socks and adjusting the fan, Cyd said she was going to explore the streets and promised to return soon. It had been a long day and I wanted to take a bath, even though we only had cold water. Shortly after she left darkness descended and I became mesmerized by the melodic Balinese chimes from the locals appeasing the Gods as sunset. The rich, full tone of each note blended together to create waves of warm, happy sounds. I laid on the bed for what seemed like hours listening to the music, when I realized that it had been some time since Cyd went out.

I knew Bali to be a safe place and wasn't really concerned about Cyd's whereabouts, when I heard a tapping at the window. When I opened the door, Cyd was doubled-over and crying, one hand clutching the keys, the other her stomach.

"What's wrong?" I asked. (I quickly checked that she still had her money belt and belongings.)

Sobbing, Cyd replied she had fallen somewhere.

"What are you talking about? Where'd it happen?" I asked, sounding more like a Gestapo agent than a concerned friend.

She didn't know. "I can remember getting dizzy . . . and I leaned against this motorcycle. Then I fell." She was crying again.

After she calmed down Cyd explained that while browsing the storefronts, thick with the smell of batik and hard woods, she became thirsty. She bought a soda from a friendly street vendor and was wandering through the maze of markets when she suddenly felt faint. "I think the bike owner helped me back to our room," she mumbled.

I looked out into the shadowy courtyard but saw no signs of anyone. Convinced that Cyd wasn't hurt or robbed, we called it a night.

As the moon rose high into the clear, starry sky, bringing the insects' songs to a crescendo, we feel asleep. Soon, however, we were jolted awake by a high-pitched staccato emanating from overhead. At first I thought the ceiling fan had broken free and shielded my face with my arm. But in the dim light I could see the fan turning slowly and realized the sound was coming from something else. Something alive.

Sitting together, straining to hear the source of the clicking, Cyd and I searched the darkness and our memory banks for clues as to what might be causing the sound.

"Bats!" I shouted, startling Cyd as much as the clicking noise had. "I think it's a bat," I said, recalling similar sounds I'd heard when two bats once invaded my third-floor apartment back home.

"Do they have bats here?" Cyd asked. She covered her head just in case.

"I'm not sure."

The thing in the dark then rattled off another round of clicks as we turned our heads back and forth like radar dishes trying to determine its whereabouts.

I put on pants and a T-shirt and went to the front desk, hoping someone could tell us what was making the noise. Luckily, I ran into Eric, a wiry young Indonesian who practiced English with a smile, and told him about the noise. He chuckled at my imitation and explained that it was probably a gecko. "No problems," he said. "They eat mosquito." Embarrassed but relieved I thanked him, and upon returning to our room assured Cyd that everything was okay. We quickly fell asleep.

The next morning we chartered a *bemo*, one of the many small pickup trucks that cart people and livestock and everything else around the island, to Ubud and the Monkey Forest. The drive out of noisy, exhaust-filled Kuta was anything but relaxing. Our driver took great pride in disobeying the few rules that apply on Bali's roads, playing chicken with just about every oncoming vehicle and paying more attention to us than the road ahead. We looked at each other as he held a steady line through the gantlet and, on several occasions, laughed out loud at the prospect of being one of three cars speeding side-by-side-by-side down the narrow two-lane road.

Outside Denpasar, the capital and transportation center of the island, we drove by a giant statue of a policeman holding a platter that contained the "wreck of the week." Our driver explained that it was used to keep drivers in check, but judging from the way he was driving, this tactic worked about as well as posting speeding fines along the highways back home.

Yet disregard for one's own welfare, or the safety of others for that matter, was a common theme we had seen throughout our travels in Southeast Asia. Not that the people didn't embrace life or enjoy living. It was just that they put so much faith in their religion and what happens *after* life, that they didn't really seem to care if you stepped in front of their car or got eaten by a shark or fell into an active volcano.

The traffic, crude housing and pollution of Kuta and Legian soon dissipated, replaced by a checkerboard of rice paddies and fish farms shimmering in the yellow morning sun. Now, far from Bali's weak ties with capitalism, we stopped at Cheluk and met with some of the villagers who carved, wove and painted for a living. I was approached by a time-worn man who sidled up to me and produced two beige and brown baskets. He said nothing.

"*Berapa harga?*" I questioned, figuring to get a better deal if I bartered in Indonesian.

"Twenty thousand rupiahs," he said in Indonesian

My eyebrows arched. "*Mahal.* Too much," I said with a wave.

Probably thinking he could make more money by speaking English, he continued. "Make with my hands." With this he turned up his palms for me to examine. From years of weaving the course hemp plant, his hands had been polished smooth. He had no fingerprints or wrinkles, not even a lifeline.

"Ten thousand rupiahs," I countered. Five dollars is fair, I thought as I closely examined the weave of the baskets.

"For my family," he whispered, tears welling in his eyes. The other villagers, who had now formed a circle around us, waited anxiously to see if their friend and fellow vendor would strike lucky.

I patted him on the shoulder and said, "Twelve thousand rupiahs." The group was silent.

He waited a moment, possibly weighing his options, then smiled and said "*Bagus*." He had accepted my offer. I reaffirmed the deal was good for both me and him. He smiled and nodded.

Driving off I waved to the group of assembled villagers with one hand, while fingering the smooth texture and intricate design of the baskets with other. For years to come the musty smell of hemp would bring a flood of memories like the look of pride, determination and then satisfaction on the man's face. For six dollars we had connected on a level that transcended centuries and borders, generations and language.

As the village and its inhabitants disappeared from our view, I thought about my own grandmother and how she was a lot like these people. Simple, highly religious and rooted in tradition. She never drove a car or flew in a plane and certainly didn't believe we could put a man on the moon even after the fact. "God would never allow it," she often would argue, refusing to look at photos of the event. In fact, when I told her I was going on the trip, Grams had a hard time grasping the magnitude of such a thing; she thought I would be back in a week or two. But that didn't surprise me; after all, her mother (my great-grandmother) had lived for 70 years with a view of the Pittsburgh skyline, yet she never ventured the six miles to get there. Ironically, though, she had left her native Italy, a child bride of 16, and traveled halfway across the world in search of a better life.

We finally arrived at the Monkey Forest, where we paid a small admission fee that covered the cost of bananas and whatever the caretaker of the grounds required. Soon we began to hear the grunts and squeals emanating from the treetops of the dark forest canopy which camouflaged the monkeys' whereabouts. We walked into the shadowy ravine and, as if on cue, members of the troop revealed themselves to us. One by one they climbed down from their stations, quietly chattering, cautious yet curious as to what goodies we might provide in return for their entertaining antics.

The forest was now serene as monkeys and visitors settled into a peaceful rhythm of getting to know each other. Some people threw peanuts from a distance, others offered hand-held bananas. Still others simply watched from the hillside as monkeys claimed their booty, made for the trees and tossed the unwanted peels and shells on us from above. It was hard to imagine that they were wild animals.

I noticed two Swedes had befriended a young monkey and were trying to playfully get rid of the little rascal. Every time they put him on a rock or a tree, he would immediately pounce on their backpacks. This game of playful tag continued for a few minutes, then one of the Swedes gently pried the monkey from his friend's backpack and politely tossed the animal to the ground. One shriek from the youngster and the trees came alive with howling and screeching monkeys. More than two dozen angry primates surrounded us, baring teeth that were capable of eating more than just nuts and fruits.

Cyd and I stood completely rigid, not knowing what to do or what not to do to incite further aggression. The Swedes, on the other hand, were not faring as well. Dominant monkeys had targeted them as perpetrators and were taking turns charging them from all sides. One Swede swung his backpack in erratic circles to ward off the attackers; his partner was not quite as fortunate. An adult male about the size of a bulldog charged from his blind side and bit him on the forearm, sinking razor sharp fangs into the Swede's pallid skin. The monkey hung there by his teeth for a frozen minute as the rest of us looked on helplessly, the trees quivering with the howl and shriek of victory.

Not sure whether we would get out without a fight, I frantically checked my day-bag for anything that might repel an angry adult monkey. All I could find was a compass, bus schedule, a wine flask and camera. Not much help against a troop of monkeys defending one of their young. Fortunately, we were soon rescued by the caretaker who had heard the commotion and came running; well, not really running. He calmly walked into the grove and instructed us all to turn our backs on the animals, explaining that we must defer to the monkeys' dominance. With this most of the monkeys retreated to their hiding places in the treetops, convinced that primeval justice had been served, and we all breathed easier. The caretaker gingerly applied some thick, amber salve to the two vampire-like puncture marks on the Swede's arm and assured him that the monkeys were not rabid. They would have to decide whether to simply forego treatment or take a chance with a Balinese doctor.

The event was rather unnerving and reminded us once again that this trip was not all fun and games. We were so accustomed to the regimented safety of the United States, with its fences and signs helping us keep our distance, that we had forgotten that wild animals are unpredictable, that when you remove bars and electrical fences, lions and tigers and bears, and even monkeys, play for keeps. You might become another link in the food chain, and if you tangle with them they'll show you what it means to be in touch with nature.

Upon emerging from the jungle shadows, we could see that our driver was still asleep in a shady patch near the bemo, so we ventured along a sandy road that led out of the Monkey Forest into the higher elevations of Ubud. We walked past glistening rice paddies and banana trees and simple huts watched over by battered, barking mongrels that prowled the perimeter. At the end of the road we were approached by a timid young man who introduced himself as Wayan Murdana. He apologized for his poor English and said he was a wood carver and basket weaver by trade. He asked if we wanted to see his home in the jungle and possibly buy some carvings. We looked at each other and followed him into the forest where colorful birds and playful monkeys blazed our path, past a stream where a withered old woman bathed under a trickling waterfall. Finally arriving at a modest hut deep in the forest, we were alone but for the screech of parrots and other exotic birds.

Wallpapered with the *Bali Post*, Wayan's modest work area was cluttered with pieces of art in various stages of completion. Assorted masks, hats and charms hung from strategically placed pegs protruding from the walls and ceiling. The tables, chairs and floor were home to frogs and dolphins and whales carved from different hard woods and painted vibrant greens and reds and blues.

His daughter, who could have passed for one of his smooth, ebony carvings, appeared from the back room of an adjacent hut. She smiled and bowed respectfully. *"Selemat pagi."*

"Pagi," we replied, and welcomed her to join us as her father selected items for our inspection. We carefully fondled each piece, tracing the intricate lines and indentations while breathing in the thick, musty odor of hard woods and dyes. After serious debate on several items, we chose a mahogany flute for Cyd's mom, who is a concert flautist, and the bargaining began. I couldn't remember what price we decided on, because at that exact moment his daughter, who had slipped away during our haggling, returned bearing the strangest gift of all. With hands cupped underneath, she gingerly presented a 35mm camera to us and asked, *"Apa ini?"* I didn't tell her right away what it was and for a moment said nothing.

Cyd and I briefly questioned each other as to how the camera might have found its way here, deep in the highlands of central Bali. Maybe a traveler lost it or had it stolen only to have the young girl find it. Maybe one of the pilfering monkeys took it and discarded it like a spent banana peel. Or maybe another visitor, overwhelmed by the peacefulness and beauty of the jungle, simply forgot it in this enchanting place.

After inspecting the equipment, we tried to explain to her father that it was a camera. We showed them how the shutter worked and they grinned and tried it themselves.

Then Wayan and his daughter and the frogs and dolphins and whales posed for a family portrait and shrieked with delight as the flash went off. But the real struggle came when we tried to explain film processing to them without opening the camera and exposing it. It was unlikely they had ever seen a film shop, and we left it at that.

When we returned along the same lazy route that we had chosen in leaving the forest, we mentally prepared for an early morning flight to neighboring Lombok Island, which promised to be a quiet, untouristed island with a wonderful mix of natural beauty and simple people. It seemed like the farther east we traveled in Indonesia, the more remote and pristine the country became, and we wanted more of what we had found at the edge of the Monkey Forest. Our confidence had grown and with it our itinerary.

We caught the earliest of the first-come, first-served flights on Merpati Air and flew over Selat Lombok. I thought about the tiny arcs we were adding to our original itinerary and how we might not get home in six months, or ever for that matter. We had been on the road for almost six weeks and were becoming more and more accustomed to simple living. I could almost hear my dad saying, "I told you you'd never want to work again." I was abruptly stirred from my daydream by the emergence of steep, green mountains ringed in clouds that allowed occasional glimpses of the approaching runway.

After landing we waited inside the one-room airport terminal, amid the smell of jet fuel and the garbled buzz of Indonesian chatter. I could see two old men struggling on the scorching tarmac to pull the cart stacked with our flight's luggage into the terminal. They left it for us to sort through like a sale bin in a department store. For what seemed like the one-thousandth time, we danced under the weight of our bags, twisting and contorting our bodies while strapping on the backpacks.

Outside, the din and putter of bemos and minibuses filled the early morning air, drowning out roosters announcing the day's arrival. A young man wearing dirty, tattered clothes stood close by and quietly offered to take us anywhere we wanted.

I said, "Senggigi Beach," confident I knew where I was going.

He thought for a moment. "Twenty thousand rupiahs," he said, testing whether I did.

"*Mahal!*" I playfully barked at his outrageous price. "How about 3,000 rupiahs?" I said.

With a thumbs-up gesture he replied, "*Bagus,*" and we loaded our packs into his dilapidated blue-and-rust Dodge Colt.

The road deteriorated with each mile we traveled away from the airport, the countryside exploding in blossoms all around us. Cattle and goats dotted the fields, while children and old women posed as question-marks stuck in the rice paddies. Tropical plants and trees gave way to azure seas crashing against rocks and sand. Our driver said little as he negotiated the hairpin turns and steep climbs along the sparsely inhabited coastline. We spied several huts among the trees betrayed only by their pathways and hanging laundry, and eventually came to the small seaside village of Senggigi.

"*Selemat tinggal,*" he said as he sped off.

"*Selemat jalan,*" we shouted into the dust and noise and exhaust from the *bemo*.

We lugged our packs to the Pondok Senggigi, an unassuming cluster of huts surrounding a garden and fountain at the base of the mountains; across the road, the sea. Friendly people who spoke tourists' English checked us in and ushered us off to our room: a clean, quiet single lodging with attached *mandi*, a small brick structure that doubled as a toilet and water catchment for showers.

We unpacked and settled into our new lodging as we had every other travel day thus far: Cyd trying to take a nap and me keeping her awake by pointing out things to do and places to go on our map. Because she couldn't sleep and I didn't want to, we compromised by taking a leisurely walk along the empty beach.

Once out in the brilliant sunshine and within earshot of the surf, we came to life, as did the urchins who systematically comb the beachhead. They appeared from nowhere: smiling, laughing, hawking T-shirts and carvings and straw hats that had seen better days. In an amebic circle they followed our trail, practicing their English, a mixture of sixth grade vocabulary and what they had picked up from intermittent contact with tourists.

An impish little boy spoke first. "Want a T-shirt, mister?"

"What's your name?" I said in Indonesian.

"Johnny," he proclaimed proudly. With that he produced an armful of T-shirts from a tattered bag.

Seeing an opening, a taller, young girl jumped in front of him, her beautiful toffee-colored skin and womanly features belying a girl her age: 12. "You pretty miss," she said to Cyd. "Pineapple?" She shoved the fruit into Cyd's face.

Others in the group practiced their English and lobbied their wares, touching our arms to see if our flesh felt the same as their sun-dried mahogany brown skin. We felt like deities as we walked among the children, swaying and stumbling in the sand as they pulled us in different directions.

One of the older boys sheepishly offered his hand to me. Long, neatly filed fingernails brushed across my palm as we shook hands. He introduced himself as Mo, short for Mohammed, and apologized for not speaking English as well as the younger children. "I'm Johnny's brother," he said. He also told us Johnny's real name was Hari. Johnny smiled and shrugged.

"We live in the south of Lombok, far from here," Mo explained. Hari nudged under his brother's arm. "We sell shirts on the beach. Hari sells the most." Mo laughed and then nodded his head at his brother. "Hari is 12 years old, but smart like 20."

"That's impossible," I said, re-examining the child who only moments ago we thought couldn't be more than seven or eight, his playful demeanor and elastic skin reminiscent of my boyhood summers in Pennsylvania.

"It's true," Mo replied. Johnny nodded.

"So how old are you?" I asked, sure that Mo was in his early teens.

Mo looked down at his long toe-nails buried in the sand. "Twenty-one," he said softly. "I'm getting married this year."

Cyd and I looked at each other and then back at the boys, who for the rest of our lives would always remain young boys with gentle mannerisms and brilliant smiles. Mo explained that his marriage had been arranged long ago and that they would live with his family until he could build his wife a home, which consisted of a thatch palm roof and wooden supports, more like a car port than a house. He then invited us to come to his village. We could stay in his home; his family would want us to be comfortable. Elated at the prospect of visiting a village, we weren't sure whether our stay would cause hardship for Mo and Hari's family. "We'll see," Cyd and I muttered. Then we said good-bye.

Once we rounded the tip of the harbor, we could see some of the resorts that were beginning to spring up and, though there weren't many, the intoxicating beatitude of the moment began to wane. At almost the same instant a fuzzy faced seaman blocked our view and offered us a sailing cruise of the harbor. I haggled with him and agreed to a fair price, whereupon he summoned his two sons, possibly ages six and ten, who I helped push our sailboat off the beach and into the clear water of the bay. Cyd jumped aboard the ant-like contraption (which spouted two pontoons to prevent capsizing), followed by me and then our crew of two. Somewhat to our surprise and dismay, the father helped raise the sail and then waved good-bye as his sons scurried about the boat, hurriedly preparing for our journey.

Now, it's a well-known fact among travelers that you tend to take a lot of risks when you travel off the beaten path, and you often do things you'd never think of doing back home: like letting two boys the same age as my niece and nephew sail our boat in the open sea. But as these diminutive sailors mastered the crude jib and tacked against the wind, I knew we were in capable hands. I also knew that Cyd was a sailing enthusiast and could save us if our sail boat ran afoul.

The wind pushed us back and forth across the mouth of the bay as our captain shouted orders to the first mate, his always-smiling younger brother. I leaned back and closed my eyes to the blazing sun, listening to the boys' musical banter and the waves lapping alongside the hull. For an hour they successfully tacked back and forth across the bay, finally depositing us safely on the shore. I thanked them both and pressed a few coins into their tiny hands.

That night we toasted our luck in discovering Lombok with a delicious candlelight dinner on the beach. For a few dollars we filled ourselves on tender garlic grouper and swordfish steaks, then retired for the evening. We awoke the next morning at 4:30 a.m. to the boastful crows of roosters, each claiming the island as its own. Waking lazily, I noticed Cyd was already awake and fumbling through her bag. "What are you doing?" I asked, clearing my throat at the same time.

"Today's your brother's birthday. I thought we'd surprise him."

I was glad Cyd remembered things like that. Throughout the trip she often called home to check in and talk to someone other than me. I had forgotten about days and dates and almost everything else back home, but I joined her in the early morning light as we searched our money belts for our AT&T calling cards. Our good mood quickly turned sour, however, as Cyd and I came to the same realization: our calling cards, along with credit cards, travelers checks and various other documents were back at the Simpang Inn on Bali (and Karl Malden was nowhere to be found). We couldn't remember all the items we had left behind, but we'd heard so many horror stories about lost passports and credit card abuses that it didn't matter if we lost an old college ID, we had to get it back.

Due to the early hour the public telephone office was closed, so we ran frantically from lodging to lodging, hoping to get a phone hookup with Lombok's more famous sister island. Our scrambling paid off when I discovered a phone at the Batu Bolong Cottages along the beach. Fortunately, I had kept as a memento a business card from the Simpang Inn, which had the phone number. I could make the call, but rousing someone who spoke enough English to discuss lost credit cards was another story. To make matters worse, we had chartered a boat to Gili Air, an even smaller island in the Indonesian archipelago with no electricity or telephones, which was due to depart at 6 a.m. We were planning a week-long stay on Gili and, since there were no regular boats from Senggigi, it was now or never.

The clerk at Batu Bolong made the connection and handed me the phone. I began my slow, deliberate attempt to describe who I was, where I was, and why I was calling. Suli, whose smile and broken English I remembered from our visit, tried to be congenial and did a good job of feigning understanding. But as friendly as our conversation was, I knew we were sunk if I couldn't talk to someone else. Meanwhile, the long-distance call was clicking the meter to the tune of 6,000 rupiahs a minute.

I told Suli to wake Eric, one of the help who I knew spoke good English, and that I'd call back in 15 minutes. He happily agreed and closed with a joyful *"Selemat jalan."* I said good-bye the old-fashioned way and hung up.

For the next 15 minutes Cyd and I tried to recount what we were missing, how the items were probably being abused and what we could do about it. Waves of questions and scenarios washed through our minds. Would someone not knowing what to do with such cards throw them away? Could they, would they, use them in a spending spree? Was another traveler on his or her way home compliments of our credit cards, or was everything tucked neatly under the mattress as we had left it? It was time to call again.

As the clerk redialed the number, Cyd went to hold the boat and secure our charter for a "few more minutes," which in Indonesia meant we had some time to play with. Cyd later told me on her return to the cottages she picked up an entourage of children offering to braid her hair or weave a cloth bracelet. They touched her sunblocked skin for good luck and told her how pretty she was. She found it hard to worry about the missing cards, and when Sebu, the brightest and most domineering of the sun-baked children, offered a pineapple she could not resist. Cyd plopped down amid a circle of laughing, jostling children. She watched as Sebu, using a large, crude knife carefully carved a checkerboard of slices into the pineapple's leathery covering and methodically peeled away pieces to reveal the luscious yellow fruit, which could be held by the stalk and eaten like cotton-candy.

Back at the cottage the number rang through to Simpang Inn, and this time I was able to talk to Eric. After exchanging amenities I explained that we had occupied Room 43 and had left belongings under the mattress. "I see," he said, and he rushed off, I presumed, to check our room. As the phone dangled on his end, the meter racked up rupiahs like a pinball machine on ours. I was certain I had told him the call was long distance, but I'm not sure he knew or cared what that meant. Frustrated and bewildered I was about to hang up when Eric returned to the phone. Excitedly out of breath, he exclaimed that he had found the items. At three dollars a minute he described them in detail, including some currencies for countries I knew he'd never see. Relieved that he had them, I let him bask in his discovery. But there was still the question of what to do in the interim. I asked if he could put them in safe keeping until we returned. "No problems," he said. "They're safe with me."

I held onto the phone for a moment after Eric hung up, then slumped against the desk. Breathing shallowly, I began to wonder why I felt a strange sense of peace. In retrospect I believe it was because I, as a once suspicious American, was becoming completely immersed in a culture where trust is implicit. For that one shining moment I believed in the best of human nature, and I have never forgotten it.

I ran to the beach where Cyd and our crew of two waited for me in the boat. "Everything's fine," I said to

Cyd's relief. Our captain grinned and we pushed off to the cheers of our little friends waving from the shore.

A Taste of the Water Island

It was on the plane headed for Hong Kong that Cyd first read about Gili Air, one of three tiny spots of sand and coral located in the Bali Sea northwest of Lombok. Now, as we skirted the coast of Lombok in a motorized canoe not much larger than a Buick, we beamed about the prospect of spending days on a coral-fringed island with no electricity, vehicles or crowds. It didn't concern us that we were carting all of our belongings in the open ocean, an ocean that once sent 80-foot tidal waves crashing into the nearby island of Flores. An ocean known for its sharks and other deep-sea creatures worthy of television documentaries. An ocean that could erase our passports and swallow our money, making it quite difficult, if not impossible, to leave the country.

Two hours after saying good-bye to Mo and Hari, maybe for the last time, we could see the charcoal slivers of the Gili Islands outlined on the horizon. The captain bragged that we were almost to Gili Meno, the small and barren central isle of the three, and that it was time to settle our account. In an instant I was transported back to the junk at Cheng Chau. I could feel the heat slowly rise in my chest and face as I recalled the Chinese pilot attempting to renege on the deal he had struck with Bill. I marveled at this universal practice of changing horses in mid-stream, or mid-strait, as was the case now.

"We want to go to Gili Air!" I said emphatically. I pointed to the tiny island that couldn't be more than a quarter of a mile away. He looked puzzled and smiled when I questioned him about our destination. Another familiar tactic, I thought. I firmly restated that we agreed on Gili Air. "You gave us your word."

Somewhat frustrated, he turned the boat and aimed it directly at the western shore of Gili Air. Triumphant, I basked in the thought that money doesn't drive all men's decisions. I also promised myself that I would tell Bill about my coup.

The captain shifted his focus from money to our new course. He negotiated several coral outcroppings, surfing in harmony with the incoming waves, and masterfully beached the boat right in front of a hand-painted sign that read: Hink Bungalows. A small group of dark men wearing colorful sarongs and bleached sandals greeted us at the beach. As they welcomed us, an older man mentioned that he'd never seen anyone come ashore like that: He thought we looked like pirates invading the island.

True to Cyd's promise, the days that followed on Gili Air were tropical paradise. We snorkeled, lazed in the sun and took leisurely strolls first clockwise, then counter-clockwise, around the entire island, which took little more than an hour. As is customary at Hink Bungalows, we sat with the villagers at the same time each day and ate three spicy meals of rice and chilies and fresh fish we occasionally saw drying on the sand. Sunset brought ceremonial offerings to the gods and ritual songs which echoed between towering Mt. Rinjani and the distant outline of Mt. Batur on Bali 100 miles to the west.

At night we sat around a bonfire with Rizal, Kadir and the other men of the village, huddled together in sarongs to fend off fleas and the night wind. We listened to tales of life in Indonesia, the hardships and political corruptness, and philosophy. The flames reflected in the blue of Rizal's eyes as he recounted his most vivid memory of "the black magic."

Hunched like a toad near the fire, Rizal told us his story. "I was at a festival," he began, "where two huge men were fighting with the rattan. You know, the sharp sticks that they tie to their hands." He made clawing gestures in our direction. "It was very hot and they were sweating and bleeding from the scratches. One man, he was winning, but then the other did the black magic."

The rest of the group remained motionless, nodding occasionally as they stared into the fire. We had come to admire Rizal, his frog-like features, worldly knowledge (no doubt gleaned from late-night talks with visitors) and his sense of humor. But this business about black magic was a bit much, I thought.

Somehow sensing our disbelief, he turned his gaze from the fire to our faces. "The man who was losing began to stare into the crowd. I thought he was staring right at me!" The others shifted nervously on their grass mats.

"Then the most incredible thing happened. The man sitting next to me, he was a big man. He began to sweat and breath heavily." Rizal was now standing, re-enacting each event as he described it. "His eyes rolled back, and I thought he was going to faint. And then the crowd roared as the man who was losing began to gain the advantage. He beat the other man over and over and finally won." Rizal sat down.

"Do you really think it was black magic?" I asked. "I mean, maybe the guy got his second wind."

The others said nothing.

Rizal grunted. Then, surveying his listeners like a scout master telling ghost stories, he continued. "When the fight ended, I turned to the man next to me . . . and he was covered in sweat, exhausted. The fighter had summoned his strength from him and now the man was acting as if he had been in the battle. It was the black magic. I'm sure of it."

We all remained silent for awhile, then, as if awakened from a trance, Rizal said he was going hunting for octopus at the reef's edge. It was low tide and the moon was bright, so it would be good for spear fishing. He walked off into the darkness, his kerosene lantern swinging in tandem with its reflection off the placid sea, a sea that for many years had kept new philosophies out and for now protected the people of Gili Air from the civilized world.

Rooster crows acted as our alarm clock as we stumbled through the morning mist to eat a hearty breakfast of eggs, rice, exotic fruits and tea with our newfound friends. Already awake for some time, the village council comprised of Rizal, Kadir, Mohammed and several other always-smiling men greeted us. After casual conversation they began to question us about the United States.

"Is New York dangerous?" Rizal asked wryly.

Mohammed chimed in: "Have you been? How big it is?"

Each man took turns playfully grilling us as we downplayed the violence in our society. Deep inside we felt embarrassed and ashamed. What I really wanted to say was that more people are killed in pedestrian accidents in New York than are murdered, but somehow it seemed inappropriate.

"Does everyone have a gun?" Kadir inquired between bites of eggs.

We hid behind mouthfuls of food.

"Do you?" one of the others added.

We knew our friends were genuinely fascinated by the concept of guns in our society, but it was difficult to discuss the issue with them. Armed with nothing more than a sixth-grade education and English they learned from travelers, the elder Indonesians saw the world in simplistic terms. "Saddam Hussein bad, US number one." To explain the whole Second Amendment thing, especially in light of the fact that Cyd and I also objected to guns, would be a fruitless task. We feebly attempted to denounce the widespread use of guns in the country, but our questioners were already on to other topics.

"Well, it's a good thing you came here," Rizal offered. "All you have to worry about are the black mosquitoes on Gili Meno. They carry the malaria."

Better than a gun, I thought.

The morning question-and-answer session ended when a handsome boy with caramel skin and chocolate eyes offered to swim with us to the blue coral. The group mumbled approvingly. Since our arrival they had spoken of the blue coral in a wondrous and reverent way, giving it the respect of a living thing, which many people often forget it is.

We hurriedly returned to our hut and began rummaging through our bags in search of swim suits and aquasocks. While digging through her pack in gopher-like fashion, Cyd accidentally nicked her thumb with a razor blade, creating two parallel cuts that would not stop bleeding. From the other side of the hut I inaudibly questioned the sanity of snorkeling with open wounds in waters that were home to sharks, pelagics and other open sea feeders. Hoping to allay my fears, I looked to Cyd for a response.

"I don't have any tampons, either," she said.

The thought of blood-lusting creatures in the sea did not seem to bother her, but it wasn't that easy for me. We left the hut and joined our guide, who had stripped to his underwear (which doubled as swim trunks) to go in search of the blue coral. We walked out through the shallows, following a sandy path carved by villagers' footsteps that wound its way among chunks of coral. I lagged behind, scanning the horizon for a fin or black blob that would allow me to tell everyone "I told you so."

When the tepid water reached our midriffs, we each submerged into a tranquil underwater world that was more like an aquarium than the ocean. I had snorkeled in Key West and the Caribbean, but it couldn't compare to the water clarity and abundance of sea life that unfolded in front of me. These waters were virtually untouched by man, except for occasional snorkeling, midnight octopus hunts and an Indonesian ceremony in which pregnant women swim under the full moon to ensure a healthy, intelligent child.

As we were swept along by the current, all thoughts of blood and sharks drifted out to sea in the surging tide. The undersea cinemascope rolled on below us, revealing wave after wave of crimson and gold, yellow and blue, a montage of coral and fish and various other things we'd never seen. Our guide effortlessly glided along, pointing out fish nibbling on smaller fish, various corals, sea anemones and a shiny blue-black sea urchin hidden among the rocks on the bottom. Cyd followed closely behind the guide as I treaded water at a distance, trying to adjust my mask.

Distracted from my mask troubles by a light tapping on the surface nearby, I could see the guide had poked his head out of the water and was motioning to me. I ducked under the surface and immediately was stunned by the vast

45

florescent field of aquamarine coral that spread before us. I had never seen that color of blue in nature before, somewhere between azure and midnight with a shimmer and sheen like velvet.

Looking in wonder at that disolving coral bed, it was hard not to believe as the Balinese do in the gods of the sea, who created such magic. Cyd and I joined hands as we floated lazily above the vibrant sea floor shining like neon in the sun's brilliant rays. That's how we spent the majority of our time on Gili Air, "the island of water."

One day while circling the island we encountered some boys who, because of the hot midday sun, were excused from chores and permitted to play in the tidal flats. Naked, they tumbled and rolled over a mound of seaweed, yelling with all their might to *Garuda*, the Indonesian god of the sky. Cyd tried to talk to them, but they were too shy or busy playing to respond, so we stood by and quietly watched.

Then, from the weeds behind us we heard giggling. We turned to see a trio of girls in red and yellow dresses passing a large wooden bowl between them.

"*Selemat sore,*" we said, and they giggled some more. Slowly we approached them as the two older girls pushed their younger sister forward

"Hi," Cyd replied with a smile. The other girls moved closer.

"Hello," the youngest one, who had bright red ribbons tied into her wavy black hair, said loudly. She took the bowl from her sisters and offered us the fruit, then rolled what looked like a small radish in a pile of coarse sugar and popped one into her mouth. To the children's delight we followed her lead. Our eyes bulged and we smacked our lips at the tartness of the fruit, which tasted like lemons and had the consistency of water chestnuts. "*Terima kasih,*" we responded with a smile, and the girls giggled approvingly.

"*Apa ini?*" I asked, hoping to discover what it was we were eating. My translation of their response was that they said "apples," but this was like no apple I had ever tasted.

46

Without sugar it would have been unbearably tart. We exchanged smiles and tidbits of simple conversation and then went on our way. It was getting late and we did not want to get caught in the darkness that would soon envelop the island. As we followed the curve of the shoreline, the sun dissolving on the distant horizon, we began to hear the ceremonial music and chanting of the islanders preparing for sundown. It was one of many rituals we had seen where the Indonesians thanked various gods for another day. We felt fortunate to be a part of it, if only for a few days, and see for ourselves how simple life could really be.

And simple was the right word. No running water. No electricity. No toilets but for a hole in the ground. And no toilet paper. But lack of quality toilet paper (which I now believe is the definitive way to measure a country's development) didn't stop us from realizing that sacrificing a few creature comforts for total freedom was a no-brainer.

We awoke the morning of our last day, the air hazy and hot even before the sun peeked over the top of Mt. Rinjani. Boarding the ferry we set off for the tiny port of Bangsal, across the surging strait that separates Gili Air and Lombok, where we would proceed overland to Senggigi. Nobody said much but Cyd, who was lamenting her run-in with a jellyfish the day before and was now examining the string of swollen welts on her knee. Without a word, Rizal pulled a hand-rolled cigarette from his pocket. He tore open the paper and removed some of his cherished tobacco, which he then soaked in sea water and carefully applied to Cyd's leg.

"*Terima kasih,*" Cyd said, adjusting her straw hat and smiling at the others on board. "It feels better already." In unison they smiled and then looked back into the deep indigo sea.

LOMBOK PRIMITIVE

The long, hot trip back to Senggigi Beach began with a ride on a *dokar*, a crude, two-wheeled cart pulled by a donkey. It was an unpleasant ride and the poor animal labored under the weight of our bodies and bags. At one point I even had to jump out and push the cart myself. Fortunately, the donkey survived the half-mile ride to the mini-bus. Once on board we proceeded on a cliff-hanging ride through the jungle, wondering whether our bags would still be secured to the roof top when we arrived (that is, *if* we arrived).

Changing over to a *bemo* in Ampenan, we shared our seats with locals who were returning home with goods such as live chickens and sacks of rice from the market. The brazen teenagers who prospected for riders clung to the outside of the pickup as a woman who looked much too old to be a mother betrayed her age by suckling a new-born opposite me. I thought about how drastic aging was in a society where children are burdened with responsibilities soon after their seventh or eighth birthday.

Passengers frequently boarded and exited as we found ourselves in a cultural revolving door, exchanging pleasantries and smiles with people who had never been off the island. I squatted in the aisle so that the women and children could have their rightful seats, and they nodded their appreciation.

We arrived in Senggigi and were greeted by the snow-white smiles of our good friends Mo, Sebu and Hari, who seemed to be everywhere. We spent several days lazing on the shore and snorkeling in the bay and then made plans to explore the inner island.

While returning from the beach one day, we met a large man named Frank (obviously his tourist-friendly name) who offered to take us to the temple at Lingsar. He said it was the only Hindu-Muslim temple in the world, and that it was guarded by eels. Unlike the Hindu populace of Bali, he explained, Lombok was predominately Muslim and practiced a religion steeped in idolatry, which meant satisfying both the gods of good and evil. (That explained all of the statues we had seen, clad in black-and-white checkerboard cloth, offerings of food and flowers wrapped in banana leaves scattered at their feet.)

As Frank began our tour, he pointed out chasms and raging rivers along the road which snaked through mountains and dense forests. He tooted his horn and we waved to playful children and women carting huge baskets of goods on their heads. When we passed in the shadow of Mt. Rinjani, Frank told of his annual exodus to the 13,000 foot peak. "It is an exhausting walk. Maybe three or four days." Frank said he had done it many times. "The rocks can cause bloody feet. It's cold. Many people fast and become hysterical, yet thousands of us make the climb every year."

The dirt road rolled on through the lush countryside until we came to an abrupt stop in what appeared to be the middle of nowhere. Frank pointed to the ornate orange-and-gray columns of a far-off structure and said that was where we'd find the temple. Like all of our other drivers and guides, Frank would offer to guard the vehicle, only to be startled out of his sleep upon our return.

Approaching the entrance we were greeted by two youngsters rolling bicycle tires with sticks. We passed by with one eye on them and the other on the menacing stone faces that loomed overhead. The stifling heat and sweet smell of orchids created a mystical aura similar to incense. A dog barked, breaking the stark silence.

A cherubic man wearing a checkered sarong appeared from under a shady tree. "You like the eels?" he asked, accurately guessing that we spoke English. "I show you." He explained that the eels in the fountain guarded the temple and, for a few hundred rupiahs, he would show them to us. He then led us to another kindly man who wrapped us in rich green sarongs. We also gave him a few hundred rupiahs as he gently tied bright yellow sashes around our waists. "This satisfies the gods," he said, "and allows you to go on holy ground."

Now in our sacred attire we approached the modest temple, which was surrounded by a moss-covered stone wall that had weathered the centuries. Inside, several fountains gurgled with mountain spring water, which we figured was where the eels lived. An angelic young girl hurriedly placed some flowers inside a vestibule as an offering and made her way by us never once making eye contact.

After a quick scan of the architecture and intricate designs, a guide crumbled some egg into the water and explained how the eels were probably full from all the eggs they'd eaten today. After a few moments, two foot-long eels sliced through the water and nipped at the yellowish flotsam just beyond his fingertips. Cyd and I looked at each other. "What do you expect for a few cents?" I said.

Suddenly, our guide leapt from his crouch with a yelp. We looked toward the water and saw a gray head the size of a softball duck back under the ledge. The guide was not injured badly, but I'm sure our uncontrollable laughter hurt more than the bite.

The rest of the day's ride revealed more scenic countryside, and later we arranged for Frank to drive us to the airport the next morning. As we rode along the twisting coastline, past the colorful Chinese cemetery and crowded markets of Ampenan, a rush of memories came to mind. I thought of the perfect white teeth of children who seldom ate sugar and dreamed of America. I laughed out loud at the memory of a rock band who had played Led Zeppelin one Friday night at the Pondok Lodge, phonetically singing *"Airway to Evan."* And I held back a tear at the thought of maybe never making it back to the simple world of Lombok or, even worse, returning to a place I wouldn't recognize.

The next day, after a 30-minute flight and leisurely cab ride, we anxiously returned to Simpang Inn to reclaim our valuables. We walked into the garden courtyard and found Eric where we had left him almost a month ago, napping behind the counter. It looked as if he had never moved. After clearing the cobwebs from his morning nap, he smiled at me knowingly and proudly produced our valuables from the safe. Everything was there, including some Indonesian currency.

"Kasih, kasih," I gushed, and handed him 10,000 rupiahs, approximately five US dollars, one month's wages to most Indonesians.

Somewhat confused and surprised, he looked at the money, holding it with two fingers as if it might bite. He looked back to me and asked, "Why is this?"

"It's for taking care of everything," I replied.

Eric shook his head and grudgingly accepted the money. I don't think his upbringing had prepared him for being rewarded for what came naturally, doing the right thing. And in all our time in Indonesia this is what surprised and awed us the most: the simple ancient ways in which Indonesians lived their lives, holding god first, family second and community third. We learned much from this country of 13,000 islands, half-a-dozen religions and a non-violent historical tradition. We learned a new, yet very old, way to live.

As I walked away from Eric that last time before heading on to new adventure, I looked back to see him slowly brushing the bills I had given him over the guest register while whispering to himself. I recalled that an old Indonesian woman once said to me that this was a good-luck gesture employed by many Indonesian merchants in hopes of inspiring the gods to bring more visitors and good fortune. I wished him that and more.

RACING THE MONSOONS

It was at this point in the journey where we had planned to backtrack through Singapore, Malaysia and Thailand, hoping to outmaneuver the monsoons and get a glimpse of one of the most ancient and mystical cultures in the world, the Hill Tribes of Chang Mai. After a brief respite in Singapore, we purchased train tickets to Butterworth, a connecting point for Bangkok on the Malay Railway which trundles along on uneven tracks dissecting peninsular Malaysia. Over the next 16 hours, we passed by villages and shanties where laundry flapped in the rush of the train. The uninhabited jungle whizzed by outside our windows, as monkeys hung in the trees and on the telephone wires running parallel to rusted rails which had survived the Japanese takeover during World War II.

Occasionally the train would stop to share the single set of tracks with another train coming in the other direction. As we waited in the stale air of the afternoon sun, enterprising young men clambered aboard, hawking

51

cartons of *nasi goreng* and *mie goreng* and other fried foods, as well as bottled water and fruit drinks. They scrambled through each car, squawking and pivoting and cajoling passengers to buy their wares, well aware of how much time they had from stopovers on previous runs. Soon the train would be on its way again and several of the roving vendors had to close their deals and jump from the slow-moving train.

It was late in the afternoon when one of the car attendants, who proudly wore a pressed, white shirt and blue overcoat with matching conductor's hat, began tuning the video-cassette recorder positioned in the front corner of the car. He backed away, satisfied that the picture was good, adjusted his hat, and went into the next car to repeat the task for a different audience.

We hadn't seen a movie in a while, so we closed our magazines and books and curiously awaited the matinee. After several trailers for what looked like amateur Malay movies, we were stunned as the title "Hamburger Hill," a US tale of the Vietnam War, flashed on the screen. It was strange to be viewing such a gruesome war film when traveling so near to Vietnam, yet the other passengers were hurriedly drawing the blinds for optimum viewing.

Cyd said she couldn't stomach the movie and decided to take a tour of the other cars. She went from one car to the next, nudging past geriatric Chinese men on their way to visit family in Hong Kong. Regal Indian women accompanying their turban-topped husbands on business looked away when Cyd approached, while groups of Malay children crawled over and around the seats their parents occupied like ants on a mound, playfully using Cyd as an obstacle to deter their pursuers.

As Cyd returned to her seat, the movie came to an end with the last of its grotesque battles. Sitting with her back to the VCR, Cyd proceeded to tell of a discovery she made during her walk. It seemed that the toilets on Malay trains have no catch basin; they empty right on the tracks. For a while we discussed whether this was a unique system dependent on monsoon runoffs or a crude method of a backward country. Agreeing that it was probably a little of

52

both, we turned our attention to the next video which was being cued up by our attendant.

I immediately recognized the opening music and shook my head in disbelief. "It's Platoon," I lamented, hoping Cyd wouldn't run for the exits. Soon we realized that these movies were chosen because they had Asian actors, a real irony considering the negative stereotype presented by most US films.

Finally we decided to concentrate on our next stop, the island of Penang, and the once lush countryside that was now scarred by man and mining as we ascended into the Cameron Highlands. Barren stretches of land were abruptly interrupted by rising rock towers adorned with mosses and lichens and brush. We made brief stops in Ipoh and Taiping and, were it not for the distant twinkle of a house light or two, we never would have known anyone lived here.

It was midnight when we arrived at the terminal in Butterworth, three hours later than scheduled, and we began the familiar ritual of gathering up our things and looking for the next mode of transportation. Outside the night air was thick and humid, and uncharacteristically quiet for a railway terminal. However, the serenity was broken when we were set upon by an aggressive taxi driver who offered to take us to Penang via the causeway. He pointed to a string of lights in the distance. For sixty Malay dollars he would save us the time and trouble of taking the torturously slow ferry and then finding transportation on the other side.

Mustering what little strength I had remaining from the long day and channeling some of the frustration that accompanies such a trip, I laughed him off and then chided him for trying to gouge us. Immediately he discounted the fare by half, but it was too late. We decided instead to join the caravan of locals and tourists who trudged silently down the steps to the ferry. From there we could see the lights of Penang across the muddy waters of the channel. Cyd took a seat on one of the wooden benches and watched over our packs, while I scanned the horizon planning our next step.

I had read that Penang was the oldest British settlement on the Malay peninsula, even older than Singapore, and it had changed little since it was first settled more than two centuries ago. The cultural and economic center of Georgetown, which occupied the northeast horn of the island, displayed a rich blend of Victorian and Chinese architecture and was host to an eclectic menu of restaurants and shops. The rest of Penang was draped in jungle and overgrowth that often gave way to majestic views of the Andaman Sea.

The ferry docked at the terminal with a thud and we again joined the mass of passengers now debarking. Tourists and businessmen commandeered most of the available taxis, so we sought an elderly gentleman astride a trishaw (half bicycle, half rickshaw) who offered to take us anywhere in Georgetown for three dollars. He didn't look strong enough to cart both of us plus our equally heavy bags, but he was already loading our stuff so we accepted.

"Any suggestions where we might stay?" I asked from inside the tiny carriage.

"Southeast Asia is good," he replied, handing us our bags which we had to cradle between our knees. "You'll like."

One look at Cyd's sleepy face gave me the answer. "Southeast Asia it is," I told the driver.

With a grunt, he stepped on the high pedal of the trishaw and, lurching over the rusted handle-bars, we started down the four-lane highway into Georgetown. Taxis and cars and buses carrying many of our fellow passengers sped by as we casually rolled along. Cyd was now wide awake and questioning our sanity, while our driver focused only on the road ahead. Safely off the main road, we had the vacant streets of central Georgetown to ourselves and settled in for a relaxing midnight tour. Between huffs and puffs the driver pointed out restaurants and unique shops as he carted his quarter-ton load.

"I lived in Penang my whole life," he told us. "Even during the Japanese time. My family live here, too." As Cyd asked him about names and ages, I wondered whether his children would have to work as hard as he did, or had he made life easier for his sons, sent them to school so that one day his grandchildren could live a better life?

Soon it began to rain, then pour, drenching our bags, the front of our legs and the driver, who wore only a soiled white tank top and flowered shorts and probably welcomed the shower. Rain pelted the tombstone gray streets as water spun off the tires like pinwheels in the faint moonlight.

Rounding a turn onto a side street, I caught a glimpse of the Southeast Asia Hotel, fronted by a large fountain with garish dragons, mermaids and flying fish. For $20 we obtained a massive room with two beds, television, climate control, hot running water and a bathtub the size of a couch. Cyd was overjoyed. I fell asleep on the giant bed listening to her rhythmic splashes in the tub.

We were awakened the next morning by thunder announcing the monsoons. While we ate breakfast near the open lobby, the rain showered plants and trickled from strategically placed fountains. Taking our plans inside, we decided to tour a museum near St. George Church, which showcased artifacts, artwork and indigenous animals. But what touched us most was a newspaper editorial from 1941 that began: "This is probably the last column I will ever write for the newspaper. These may be the last words I ever write. The Japanese invaded Georgetown today."

After a quick inspection of Ft. Cornwallis, originally built by the island's founder, Francis Light, we hopped on the No. 83 bus for the airport and the Snake Temple, which was reputed to have various asps that were drugged to keep them passive. The temple was just what you'd expect of a tourist trap: A photographer offered to take your picture with poisonous snakes coiled around your neck and arms and anywhere else you'd like to hang them. We chose not to tempt fate and resumed our bus ride around the island. If we had known what lay ahead for us, we might have stayed with the snakes.

It had stopped raining and the sun bore down on us from behind a thin veil of clouds as we waited along the road for the next bus. We boarded and took our seats as the bus grudgingly pulled away from the muddy berm. A chunky Chinese official selling tickets asked where we wanted to go and I responded, "Balik Pulau," which is a small town on the other side of Penang.

"Wha you wan?" he asked, his faced contorted with confusion. He gave the lady behind us change.

"I'd like two tickets to Ba-leek Poo-lao," I said, not entirely sure of the pronunciation.

"No unerstan," he replied sharply. "Where you go?"

Now the entire bus was looking at us. I was flushed with anger and embarrassment at his unhelpful attitude. I attempted several more times to explain where we were going, altering my pronunciation in hopes he would understand, when the woman behind us offered to act as an interpreter. I paid the Chinese man two dollars for our tickets and thanked the woman, as our ungrateful ticket-taker grunted and moved on to his next victim. To this day I believe he understood me completely. I think, in a sadistic way, he enjoyed belittling me in front of the other passengers. This episode re-emphasized something we hadn't cared to learn about the world: There is no monopoly on ignorance.

Meanwhile, the bus had found its way into the verdant heart of Penang, alternately scaling tree-lined peaks and tracing the jagged shoreline below. Nondescript villages appeared and disappeared without warning, welcoming home passengers after a hectic day in the markets of Georgetown. The bus finally dropped us off in Balik Pulau and we wandered around the plaza and shops until the next bus came.

Whining and grinding, the connecting bus began the slow ascent back over the mountain along a series of hairpin turns and switchbacks. It was late in the day and our driver was making good time, haphazardly bouncing the bus off of hillsides and clipping tree limbs on his last route of the day. Branches from exotic trees and plants snapped in through open windows, shredding leaves and twigs in our hair and filling the bus with aromatic fragrances from unfamiliar flowers.

Most of the passengers had debarked and, except for the rattle of cans tumbling around the floor and the snoring of the sadistic ticket-taker, we were alone on a speedy sightseeing tour of the island. From my window I could see several smaller islands dotting the Andaman Sea below, and I wondered what was the next body of land beyond them. Just then the bus careened off a wayward boulder alongside the road, bouncing us from our seats and sending the ticket-taker sprawling onto the floor. From the corner of my eye I could see his embarrassment, and I chuckled out loud. Instant Karma, I thought.

Back at the hotel, Cyd filled the tub with steaming hot water while I lazed in the coolness of our room watching a soccer game on the television. I drifted off to sleep wondering what everyone was doing back home and whether I could ever retain my previous lifestyle, or rather, whether I wanted to.

Later that night we met a German student traveling alone and asked him to dine with us at Dawood's, a popular Indian restaurant we had heard about in Singapore. Between bites of spicy beans and potatoes and *curry kapitan* (a chicken dish that got its name from a Dutch seaman, who in response to the captain's request as to what was for dinner, replied "Curry, Kapitan"), this young man admitted that he really didn't like Americans. When asked why he said, "I don't know. I just don't." We bought him dinner anyway.

His comment reminded us again how people from the United States get a bad rap when traveling, some of it probably deserved. We're rich and demanding, and think that the rest of the world should cater to our beck and call. But throughout our trip we made a concerted effort to avoid being "ugly Americans." If anything, we probably kept to ourselves a bit too much.

Wandering the alleys and back streets, we later stumbled upon an outdoor Chinese theater and several shops and restaurants that we promised to visit in the days ahead. But first we had to get through the monsoons which returned with a new vengeance and trapped us along the grid of walkways that crisscross throughout the city. Sitting under a decrepit overhang, we watched the streets fill up with water, empty but for an occasional brave soul who would sprint by in random splashes and the tireless trishaw drivers carting half-soaked passengers to their destinations.

BIKES TO BELLEVUE

The day started with a brilliant blue sky and sultry breeze that dismissed all thoughts of clouds and downpours. We were soon on our way to Penang Hill (a 2,400-foot-peak that overshadows the island) on rented bikes that looked like rusty remnants from British colonial times. Though we had experienced left-side driving while in England, it is a lot different when you're peddling a rickety bike through the exhausts of speeding cars and motorbikes. Eventually we made it through the gantlet and arrived at the foot of Penang Hill and its sixty-degree funicular railway, compliments of Swiss engineering.

During the steep climb aboard the rail car a Malay gentleman, sporting a variety of gold chains and pendants, asked where we were from. "What do you do there?" he asked in rather good English.

"We used to be in advertising," Cyd replied. "But now we're changing careers. I'm going to be a teacher when we get back."

"Very good," he replied. "The world needs more teachers."

That's what Cyd thought, too. In the weeks prior to our departure, amid the welcome zaniness of preparing to leave, Cyd decided that teaching would be a rewarding profession. A welcome change from the business world. She applied to the University of Pittsburgh in hopes of enrolling upon our return. Me, I had no idea what I would do, nor did I care at this point.

Cyd commented on how well the man spoke English, and he thanked her. He then proceeded to tell us that Malays receive a good education by Asian standards. "Much better than my brothers in Indonesia," he continued. "They only attend the sixth grade, which

58

makes it difficult for them to get ahead." They continued talking as I turned my thoughts to Hari and Mo, and how they might never leave Lombok.

The car stopped halfway up the hill among some boulders the size of houses and strained against gravity to allow the gold man and his gang of laborers to exit. "*Selemat jalan,*" the man shouted over the screech of wheels as we started upward again. "And good luck."

"*Selemat tinggal,*" Cyd replied, waving good-bye as the men faded out of view.

By the time we reached the summit the sky had become overcast and an eerie silence enveloped us as we walked the remaining pathway to the peak. In the distance Georgetown stretched to the horizon like a 3D postcard. Ships appeared frozen in the channel as we strained to detect the sound of horns or revving engines that pervaded the miniature streets and houses far below. We reveled in the silence.

After a brisk walk we settled in for lunch at a tiny garden cafe overlooking the city and miles of mainland Malaysia that pushed far to the north. Snacking on butter-bread and tea, we listened to caged birds whistle and chirp while the mist drifted in through the doorway. A rose trellis framed the distant matrix of streets and houses comprising Georgetown, which was about to get an afternoon dowsing. The clouds rolled in and we could hear toucans, parrots and a rainbow of other exotic birds throughout the Bellevue Aviary singing in the mid-day shower. It was late in the afternoon when the incline came to a safe stop at the bottom of the hill and we were soon on our way back to Georgetown.

BANGKOK OR BUST

The next day we left Penang for Hat Yai, a nondescript border town where we'd have our passports validated for travel in Thailand, and then it was overnight to Bangkok. We were lucky to get the last two first-class tickets, which meant we would have air-conditioning and sleeping berths (and hopefully no videos) for the 20-hour trip.

The stopover at Hat Yai gave me a chance to befriend a young man who looked American and, as it turned out, was from Canada. He was living in Bangkok, teaching English on the sly, and I asked his help in pronouncing some Thai words.

"Your numbers are fine," he said, after I did some counting. "But you've got to be more nasal."

"More nasal!?" I questioned in my best whining voice.

He laughed and shook his head. Then he quickly turned away, acting as if he didn't know me.

I thought maybe I offended him with something I'd said.

"I have to be careful," he whispered as one of the attendants left the car. "Every month I leave the country and re-enter to validate my passport. I don't want to draw unnecessary attention."

I remembered that Bill and Christie also practiced this game of passport roulette, making day trips to Macao and China every-so-often to renew their passports, and I understood his concern.

Not thinking clearly, I tried to change the subject to more mundane topics. "So, where do you teach in Bangkok?" I asked, as another attendant passed by.

The Canadian turned pale. He quickly shot back that he didn't live in Bangkok, making sure that the attendant heard him. I again apologized for my gaffe, but he dismissed it with a wave and pointed out more nuances of the language. "Because you're a male," he explained, "you have to add *khrap*, you know, like shit, when saying thank you."

Chuckling, I took the opportunity to practice by repeating *"Khop khoon khrap"* over and over as I returned to my seat.

Now content that I had mastered some simple Thai phrases, I began to wonder what was happening to my brain. Had my mind atrophied to the point that I was having an easier time speaking Indonesian and Thai than my native tongue? It seemed the longer I was away from work and the demanding pace of living in the United

States, the constant sources of stimuli, the more my thinking slowed. It got to the point that Cyd and I would laugh at how strange we sounded, often dropping letters and words to communicate like the indigenous people we met.

By now the line through immigration had thinned and Cyd took my place guarding our bags. It's a tragic reality that you have to protect your valuables in most developing countries, but I guess that's better than having to protect yourself. Not once in all our months of travel did we ever fear for our safety, and it was no coincidence that most of the countries we visited had rigid gun laws. Other than an outright war or coup, we had little to worry about in the way of gun play.

Outside in the ever-present drizzle that we had become accustomed to, I waited with a few soldiers, nationals and tourists. A few auburn Malay women in weathered sarongs peddled fried foods and corn-on-the-cob that had obviously been cooked over an open flame. Finally, one of the stoic officials behind the counter stamped my passport allowing me to leave Malaysia. Then I walked across the border to have another official permit me entrance to Thailand.

From Hat Yai we slowly made our way toward Bangkok, following the curve of the gulf coast and then negotiating the narrow parcel of land that runs for miles along the Burmese border. My neck hurt from peering out the window for long periods of time at the stunning panorama, a beatific landscape that one would never suspect was home to ruthless drug-runners and sporadic guerrilla operations. I told myself that this is what Vietnam must have been like, and maybe still was, and turned my attention back to a forgettable little book that I never finished reading.

Nightfall came quickly and the attendant broke down the seats to produce our sleeping berths, complete with crisp white sheets and down pillows. The rocking of the train put me to sleep almost instantly, while Cyd read one of the hundreds of magazines and books she devoured during the six-month period. Sleeping in the top berth reminded me of fall days of my youth when we used to ride out the wind in my friend's tree house. And to think I had agreed to let Cyd have the bottom berth so she could answer nature's call in the middle of the night.

Our strategy paid off in the wee morning hours when Cyd clambered out of her lower berth in search of the toilet. In the ghostly light of the rail car, Cyd tip-toed past each compartment, seemingly unoccupied but for snoring and an occasional foot sticking out from behind the curtain. She slid open the door that led to the next car and was greeted by a warm rush of air and night wind. Closing her eyes, she balanced herself in the doorway, listening to the rattle and click-clack of steel against steel as the train rolled along the tracks. Caught up in the moment, Cyd failed to notice the mound of bodies huddled at her feet, passengers too poor to afford berths and seeking the common bond of keeping each other warm. Startled at first, she smiled at the young men pressed together like spoons and carefully stepped over them and into the next car. Cyd had become accustomed to many things during the trip, but peeing on the tracks was something she never got used to doing. Soon she returned to her berth, sidestepping the huddled mass now facing the other direction, and pulled the chain to turn out the light.

It was Labor Day back home. We awoke to the familiar morning scent of juice, toast and fruit, which was being served by our ever-present attendant. I pulled back the curtains and was greeted by the early morning sun and row upon row of crowded markets set against the rich greens of the countryside reflecting a silver coat of dew in the dawn light. Thai women and men adorned in colorful sarongs sifted through huge, makeshift bins containing vegetables and fruits that had been carted overnight from the outlying farms beyond the verdant backdrop. As I dressed and ate breakfast I couldn't tear myself away from the silent documentary slowly rolling along outside my window, which now showcased thousands of crude metal lean-tos and miles of hopeless slums that announce one's arrival to cities like Jakarta, Bombay and Bangkok.

At the train station we were gathered up by a frenetic Chinese cab driver who took us on a whirlwind tour of the city. His route doubled the distance to our hotel (fortunately I had negotiated a set price beforehand), as he unsuccessfully attempted to avoid the morning traffic jams. But that was just an appetizer. In the days ahead we found Bangkok to be one continuous choking rush hour after another. In fact, one driver told us that the city was planning to void all existing cab licenses to lessen the traffic volume (which was estimated to contain as many as 10,000 illegally operating cabs) and reissue new ones to legitimate owners.

Our final destination, The Miami Hotel, was an oasis amid the urban noise and pollution outside. The Chinese women at the front desk, though stoic, were very accommodating and helpful, and that was more than we could say for most of the people we met on the street. It seemed like every time we asked directions or hailed a cab in the city, we wound up in the wrong place asking directions of someone else that eventually led us to a different place. This scenario repeated itself throughout our entire stay in Bangkok which was partly due to my butchering of the language and the Thai people's limited understanding of English. It made the city seem a lot hotter and more congested than it actually was.

Yet our greatest frustrations came whenever we flagged down a *tuk-tuk* (took-took), the souped-up golf carts that buzzed around the city at high speeds, spewing noxious fumes and terrorizing pedestrians. On more than one occasion we negotiated a price for one destination, only to be carted to various jewelers, stores and clothiers to sample their goods instead.

One particularly hot and humid day (which describes just about every day in Bangkok) we hooked up with a charismatic young *tuk-tuk* driver. He raced through bumpy alleyways and over bridges spanning the muddy *klongs* that form a watery spider web around Bangkok, while telling us the secret to driving in the city. He explained that *tuk-tuk* drivers often worked in tandem with local businessmen, and if the passengers they brought in browsed long enough in the shop, or even better, if they bought something, the driver was compensated with a gas coupon by the merchant. This strategy brought more customers into the store, put gas in the driver's tank and gave tourists the ride of their life. "All very good for the economy," he said.

Trusting our newfound friend, we availed ourselves as shills in return for a ride to a soccer match at the stadium. He took us on a whirlwind tour of the city, collecting enough gas coupons along the way to last the week, while giving us a chance to see a lot of the city, albeit at breakneck speeds. The *tuk-tuk* finally skidded to a halt in a cluster of shops that looked like all the others in Bangkok, and our driver said we could get out there. When we asked where the stadium was, he pointed in no particular direction and sped away. Cyd and I looked at each other and realized that we were at almost the exact same place where he had picked us up.

It was noon and the sun curdled the chocolate floodwaters of the Chao Phraya River as it slopped over the uneven river banks bordering Bangkok's western limits. Exhaust fumes and rancid stench from grease and open sewers made us lightheaded, along with the prospect of walking in the intense heat. But Bangkok never stops, and it wasn't long before we were zooming up Rama I Road in an air-conditioned cab. We arrived at the national stadium and bid our driver farewell. The lack of crowds, noise and fervor associated with Thai soccer matches led us to realize that once again we had been misinformed. Guards outside the gate told us there was no match today; in fact, the season had ended weeks ago. We laughed and hailed another cab for the ride back to our hotel.

Along the way we recounted one horror story we'd heard from travelers that made our run-ins with scheming *tuk-tuk* drivers pale greatly in comparison. While staying on Lombok we befriended a Canadian couple who had made their way through Thailand before coming to Indonesia. We gave them the tip to visit Gili Air and they imparted words of wisdom about Bangkok that I would never forget. Taking a similar hiatus from their lives, they had flown from Toronto to Bangkok and were in the city only a few days when they encountered a friendly Thai merchant on the street. He took them to visit *wats* and temples obscured by the modern buildings around Bangkok and offered advice on where to dine and stay during their visit.

One morning he showed up outside their hotel and offered to take them to a jeweler who, because he was a close friend, would also give them a great price on opals. Being young and naive and full of the freshness of their journey, they agreed to take advantage of his generous offer. They gave the merchant $500 for several opals that would be delivered to their hotel the next morning. After waiting some time for their "friend" to show up, they decided to return to the jeweler and personally pick up the gems. When they arrived at the store, the building was empty and there was no sign of the merchant or his friend.

But the misfortunes of a few careless travelers didn't mean that everyone in Bangkok was a con-artist or cheat; on the contrary. Most of those we met in the markets and back streets were hard-working, everyday people who, were it not for their sing-song language and caramel skin, would be right at home on a farm in Iowa.

Later that night we inquisitively meandered along Patphong Road, leading to Bangkok's renowned sex and sin center, which had nothing on Times Square or Hollywood Boulevard. Yet I couldn't help but notice the excessively young age of the girls, who are often sold by their families like livestock to help make ends meet. I later discovered that Bangkok also has one of the highest rates of heterosexually transmitted AIDS.

After a few awkward minutes of politely turning down advances from young women and girls, we stumbled upon a quaint French cafe and dined on veal cutlets and steak filets, topped off with fine wine and strawberry cheesecake all at a reasonable cost. Intoxicated with the wonderful meal and cool night air, we took a relaxing after-dinner stroll before calling it an evening. I waved to a *tuk-tuk* driver headed in the other direction and watched in amazement as he circled without braking and screeched to a halt in front of us.

Cigarette dangling from his lip, he asked us where we wanted to go. I told him the Miami Hotel, which he recognized and claimed would cost 60 baht, or roughly three dollars. I wasn't in the mood for haggling, but it was customary and, hey, the drivers got a kick out of it.

"Thirty baht," I responded, halving his initial offer.

He ran a handful of spindly fingers through his greased back hair and replied, "Fifty baht."

"Forty," I said, and began to walk away.

"Okay, okay. Forty baht," he hollered, raising four fingers to make sure I understood.

We jumped aboard the blue-and-yellow *tuk-tuk*, ducking under the garish tassels that hung from the roof, and landed on the rock-hard seat with a thud. In an instant we were streaking toward our destination, our driver singing and laughing maniacally as he alternated between throttle and clutch.

We were either too drunk, stunned or caught up in the moment to care that this guy was out of control, but when we arrived safely at the hotel, I tipped him a couple of baht. He looked puzzled but took the money anyway, howling over the roar of the *tuk-tuk* as he sped away.

A VISIT FROM THE KING OF SIAM

Midway between Bangkok and Cambodia there lies an island paradise called Koh Samet. It is relatively free of tourists and development that plague many other parts of the world. Yet life there is a paradox. Sugary sand hosts voracious fleas. The warm waters provide great visibility, but host very few fish. The island is made up of axle-snapping dirt roads and jagged rocks that conceal desolate, exotic places to explore. And, as I would soon find out, its serene setting was not the place to be sick.

The day after arriving on the White Shark Boat from Ban Phe, I began to experience intense headaches, which for me could mean only one thing: constipation. After sampling some *kaeng kari kai*, a volatile curry chicken dish which I ate for lunch, I quickly ruled that out. I took a couple of Tylenol and blamed the pain on the rigors and blue-green haze of Bangkok's concrete jungle. In a few days I would be fine.

That night I awoke, soaking wet and shivering like a stray Thai cur. My skull was pounding and it hurt to look in any direction without first turning my entire head. I put on a dry shirt, popped two more Tylenol, and went back to sleep. The next morning, I awoke to more of the same. I began to wonder whether I had contracted dengue fever or, worse, malaria while in the wilds of Indonesia.

I ran my half-baked hypothesis by Cyd, who assured me I was okay and that I would feel better if I went swimming. Since I felt like I was on fire, it seemed like a good idea at the time, yet the coolness of the water provided only temporary relief. In addition, I found swimming to be hard work. Cyd, on the other hand, with her long legs and strong shoulders, glided effortlessly through the water. In harmony with the sea, she became part of the ebb and flow of the tide. She was a graceful dolphin and, like the bottom-feeding crab, I could only watch in envy as she swam by.

Once back at our hut, the pounding in my head resumed at a more pronounced level. I tried to lie down, but that caused me to be nauscous. Standing made me weak, eating made me tired. Nothing made sense. I spent the entire day reading *The Winter of Our Discontent* and watching Cyd splash like a cheerful mermaid in the undulating surf. As night approached the demons inside my skull blended the misgivings of Steinbeck's character with my own life. At times my heart raced at the thought of being found out, only to realize that I wasn't Ethan Hawley, the fictional protagonist in the book. I got up and took a cool shower and then drifted off to sleep, dozing somewhere between dreams and semi-consciousness. Soon, the bespectacled King of Siam, whose likeness was plastered on every Thai monetary denomination, invaded my dreams, dancing in and out of my head in time with the pounding that had returned. I awoke chilled and feverish.

In my deluded state I began to shower by flashlight. The cool water soothed my burning skin and took my mind off the illness for awhile. Feeling better, I looked down to see what I thought was a piece of leaf or dirt lodged between my toes. I tried to flick it away, only to discover that is was a black fungus. I started to cry. How could I have something growing there, between the piggy that went to market and the one that stayed home, and not notice it? Had I truly lost my mind?

Cyd was now awake and tried to comfort and console me, applying a wet sock to my steaming forehead. She suggested that we return to Bangkok the next morning, but first she wanted me to take an aspirin. Like a sacrificial lamb, I consented.

Maybe Buddha was smiling on me that night. Or possibly some of the orange-robed monks we passed along the beach earlier in day had said a prayer for me. Or maybe my imagined bout with malaria was cured by a sample pack of Bayer Aspirin. No matter. Morning came and the fever was gone.

We were never sure what had caused the illness (it was probably sun stroke or an allergic reaction to anti-malarials), but as quickly as it came, it went. I finished my book and felt very much alive. I was glad that unlike Ethan Hawley, who Steinbeck had take his own life, my troubles could be dismissed so easily.

GARBAGE BAGS AND WATER BUFFALOES

Throughout our travels Cyd had a knack of testing the waters, so to speak, of each country we visited. Unlike the United States and some of Europe, we found the water in the rest of the world was filled with micro-organisms and filthy additives that just didn't sit well with us. We had to drink bottled water almost everywhere we went and at no time in my life have I ever craved a glass of water as much as during the trip. We also learned that our bodies had become somewhat less tolerant of unhealthy microbes probably because we use fluorides and other chemicals to combat pollutants. Combine all of these facts with Cyd's penchant for ice-cold drinks, and it was easy to see how she would wind up with a case of King Rama's revenge. Her worst bout came the morning of our flight out of Bangkok when she awoke with stomach cramps, diarrhea and a pounding headache. I wasn't feeling 100 percent either, but we managed to stumble into a taxi and cruise along the highway to the airport.

Fortunately, our flight along the east coast was smooth and Cyd was able to sleep. I was glad she couldn't see the stream of pollutants that spilled out from the mouth of the Chao Phraya River south of Bangkok. The residue formed an unreflective lake of brown, orange and black that invaded the sparkling chartreuse waters of the gulf.

Within an hour we were banking left in the direction of a string of tropical islands emanating from the Thai-Malay border. The lush mountains of Koh Samui filled up my window, and I quickly woke Cyd to explain our windfall. Originally our plans called for us to fly to Surat Thani, a tiny transit stop, and then catch the bus to the port of Ban Don. There we would depart on a three-hour boat crossing to Koh Samui. However, in the two years since our guidebook was published, an airport was completed on Samui that allowed direct flights from Bangkok. I was glad that we were visiting, because direct flights would almost certainly turn Samui into another Phuket (a popular tourist destination on the west coast), which one traveler we met described as "Bangkok by the sea."

Shortly after arriving on Koh Samui, we stowed our bags at our hotel and jumped aboard a *songthaew* (pronounced song-tow), which was nothing more than a gaudily decorated pickup truck with two benches in back. It was headed for Na Thon, the port village on the west coast. From there we hiked more than a mile; first along the asphalt road and then into the jungle blanketing the hillside which cradled the Had Lin waterfall.

The path wound on interminably upward through dense exotic flora and always within earshot of the stream leading to its source and our destination. Occasionally we surprised some bathers or clandestine couples, nodded apologetically, and continued on and upward. About halfway up the hill we came across a hut where the owner's pet monkey was chained like a watchdog. I recalled our encounter in the Monkey Forest and, after giving this one a wide berth, we continued our climb.

Finally we reached the waterfall and were pleasantly surprised that no one was there. Well, no one but the enterprising Thai boy who sold cold water and sodas and spoke fairly good English. Time and time again I marveled at the ingenuity and hard work that people exhibited throughout our travels. I tried to envision this frail youngster hauling ice and drinks up the mountainside so he could make a few baht. Was he saving for school? Marriage? Did he have to share his earnings with his family? All of these questions coursed through my mind as I asked for a Pepsi.

We finished our drinks and tightroped over the wooden planks that served as a footbridge across the stream. At the base of the waterfall we found a muddy pool and immediately jumped in to cool off. Our playful splashing was interrupted by the emergence of another foreign couple. After exchanging greetings with them (they were from Austria), we struck up conversation about world events. It was difficult to stay abreast of what was going on in the rest of the world, and we were anxious to hear more about the *Bali Post* headline that screamed "Gorbachev" and nothing else we could decipher in the streets of Kuta. Relieved that we were not on the fringe of another world war, we turned to travel stories about unique places to go and things to avoid. "Like the water here," the woman said. "It's full of leeches."

Cyd and I smiled and judiciously scanned our extremities for "little brown slimy things," which is how I think the woman had described them. We found none. Convinced that we were leech-less, I decided to join John in climbing the waterfall, while Cyd and Kathy chatted below. I was still not feeling well and the mid-day heat wasn't making things any easier. The climb was steep and slippery, but we scratched and clawed our way to the top for a wonderful view of the valley and some refreshing breezes. I scaled a few smaller falls upstream and then took a rather bumpy route back to the bottom.

Cyd and I bid our newfound friends good luck and good-bye and started back down the hillside. As we neared the end of the path, I felt an itching in my pants and immediately thought of the leeches. Without reservation I dropped my shorts and began scanning my crotch for the buggers. Cyd, who I thought would post as lookout, could only stare in amazement, until I told her why I was looking. Like baboon mates we then began to preen each other in search of unwanted guests which, to our relief, again proved fruitless.

Now back on the road to Na Thon, we found ourselves on a collision-course with steel gray storm clouds rapidly moving our way. Even though it wasn't monsoon season on the east coast, we knew that Thailand could get torrential rains at any time of year, especially in the late afternoon. We were hot and tired and thirsty and figured the rain would be refreshing, so we resigned ourselves to walk the mile or so to Na Thon and take a *songthaew* back to our room at Smile House. About halfway to the village, the rain and thunder and lightning joined hands to thwart our progress. Cyd and I argued about taking cover on a nearby porch or under a tree, while the rain, which was blowing sideways, soaked us down to our passports. We continued to bicker in the downpour, when a short Thai woman and her three children approached us wearing garbage bags as rain gear. They offered us their home-made ponchos and smiled when we waved them off, continuing on their way like a mother duck with ducklings in tow.

The rain subsided enough for us to continue walking. We met an elderly man leading a water buffalo by a rope and iron ring attached to its nose. We said hello and stared after the man and his enormous pet as they passed by. I looked the great gray beast in the eye, a slick, black marble dotting its massive horned head. In an instant I knew why a water buffalo was considered a sign of prestige and power for a Thai man.

The rain began anew and we wondered if we'd ever get dry again. As we huddled for warmth a motorcyclist appeared out of the curtain of rain and in choppy English asked if we wanted a ride. He wore a faded cotton jacket with the letters TAXI inscribed on the back, so we took him up on his offer. As we pulled out I couldn't help but think of my insurance policy, which covered injuries as a result of parachuting or bungy-jumping, but did not cover motorcycle accidents. Cyd clung to me and I to the driver, who must have sensed our apprehension and fatigue. He carefully negotiated the turns and descents along the roadway to the village where we were staying. Safe at last at the entrance to Bo Phut, we waved good-bye and wandered past the pier where the last flamingo-pink reflections of the sun winked goodnight through the dissipating clouds.

HALFWAY HOME

As difficult as third-world travel was for us, we ached at the thought of leaving Southeast Asia and the Indonesian Archipelago. Our visitor's visa for Thailand had expired, so we flew from Koh Samui to monsoon-soaked Phuket, then on to Singapore, where we finally got to see the newly renovated Raffles Hotel. While in Singapore, we got haircuts and bought magazines and caught up on world events. Cyd also got treatment for a recurring ear infection from a doctor who spoke little English but prescribed an effective cure, ear drops. Our last night in Singapore was spent wandering around the city and harbor, sampling spicy satays and drinking Tiger Beer at the outdoor hawker shops.

The next morning the bus picked us up one block from Raffles Center and moved out of the city limits toward Jurong Park and the airport. We checked our bags at the ticket counter and munched on baguettes and cheese while waiting for the plane. I looked at Cyd sitting across the table, tan and lean and unencumbered by life, and thought how lucky I was to have met her; how lucky we were to have met each other. I also wondered whether I would have taken a trip of this magnitude if our paths hadn't crossed.

The flight to Hong Kong was short by comparison to our other trip segments and we spent the early afternoon skirting the coast of Vietnam. It was a clear sunny day and I found it hard to imagine that we were flying in air space that at one time was filled the roar and thunder of fighter planes, where flak and dense smoke once obscured the ever-advancing Mekong Delta as it strained to escape the blood and death draining into its tributaries. I could not see how such a tiny, undeveloped nation could be the catalyst for a decade of senseless destruction and loss of life. During the 20 minutes or so it took to navigate the coastline, I never once took my eyes off the long stretch of jungle concealing the scars of battle and embarrassment with a canopy of new life.

Upon arrival in Hong Kong we learned that it would cost us $40 to leave and re-enter the airport. Our connecting flight wasn't for 10 hours, so we caught a cab to Hong Kong Central and cooked a dinner of spaghetti and meatballs for our friends. We shared some wine and pictures with them and they commented how nice it would be to visit Bali before returning to the States. I also told Bill about my negotiating tactics in the Lombok Strait. It was good to see them again, but we knew it was only temporary. As evening crept across the harbor, casting a blue-gray shadow on the skyscrapers of Hong Kong, we said good-bye to our friends and left *"Num bah two, say mo do"* for the last time.

CHAPTER 3 ───────────────

THE WONDERFUL WORLD OF OZ

The long flight to Sydney gave us plenty of time to catch up on our sleep, to dream about what we might do in the months ahead and to reflect on what we had done. It had been three months since I last stood in front of the giant world map adorning a wall where I worked, secretly tracing the route we had chosen and wondering how and when I would announce my resignation. Cyd had had a much more difficult time leaving the intimacy of the small agency for which she worked and flourished the past seven years. Her co-workers and clients had become friends, and she wrestled with the prospect of betrayal and hurt feelings and starting over in a new career. But that was the past.

As the plane touched down in the morning sunshine, we talked quietly about the two months we'd spend touring eastern and central Australia, which we would eventually cover by bus, plane, four-wheel-drive vehicle and a lot of trekking. After successfully retrieving our bags, the terminal doors slid open and Australia greeted us with a refreshing gush of spring air, announcing the second part of our journey. Somehow we had imagined the first segment of the trip to be spiritual and ethnically diverse, while the remainder would be more idyllic and awe-inspiring.

We breathed in the cool, dust-free air and basked in the chill of the morning as we read through mounds of literature promoting inexpensive lodging around Sydney. We opted for the Alfred Park Hotel because of its central location to the train and then boarded the first of dozens of buses that would be our primary mode of travel Down Under. It was fitting and ironic that we would spend interminable hours over the next two months following yellow dirt roads while exploring the land commonly referred to as Oz.

During our bus ride from the airport to town, we questioned the driver about the dangers for which

Australia is renowned. "What about dengue fever?" I asked. "Are there really a lot of poisonous snakes?" Cyd said. "How about the flies?" To these and other questions the driver had one response: "No worries." It was the first of many times we would heard this simple phrase, a favorite Aussie response to any and all difficult situations. It was a saying we would come to adopt as our travel credo.

Using Sydney as a base of operations, we spent the first few days touring the National Museum, harbor zoo and Sydney's renowned opera house, and felt very much at home. Maybe it was the variety of friendly people or the city's proximity to water, but in many ways Sydney reminded us of our home, Pittsburgh.

One day, at the advice of a man we met along the Circle Quay, we set out for a picnic at the Royal National Park, a large protected area of forest and dunes only an hour by train from Sydney. The train deposited us at Crunulla, a small town reminiscent of Ellesmere Port, and we lounged on the pier in the almost-too-bright sun while waiting for the afternoon ferry. Once we were on board, the bulky green-and-yellow boat pushed against the wind and waves that had picked up as we left the harbor. A sailboard rider sped along in the other direction, a triangle of red-and-black synthetics streaking across the tiny whitecaps highlighting the water. The wind reached up under my jacket and for a moment I enjoyed being cold. Maybe it was my body's way of saying that I should be preparing for winter, which was usually the case this time of year north of the Equator.

We docked at Bundeena and meandered through the scenic, uncluttered streets in search of the park entrance. A sun-scarred octogenarian, wearing a faded fishing cap to deter further skin cancer, pointed us in the right direction. He also told us to keep our eyes open for Aboriginal rock carvings.

I found it interesting that in this country, the size of the US with only one-eighth the population, even the cities were surrounded by pristine, natural environs. Ancient remnants of indigenous people were commonplace, signs of civilization scarce, wildlife such as kangaroos, wallabies and parrots abundant.

Once under cover of the brush, I changed into long pants to fend off the ticks, dried straw grass and stickers draped over the pathway ahead. I thought about our first bush walking experience. The Aborigines say that when a person needs to think clearly and get away from it all, striving to find an inner peace and oneness with nature, he or she goes *walkabout*. We forged ahead not knowing or caring where we were going, content to take in the surroundings as it came up to greet us.

We walked for miles, escorted by the sounds of the shore and often with the skyline of Sydney on the distant horizon, pausing to watch the surf crash into cavernous cliffs which dropped unexpectedly from the sandy path into the sea. Returning to the bush, we climbed several dunes dotted with scrub grass and thorny bushes forming what appeared to be numerous trails and offshoots. Thinking about nothing in particular and enjoying the walk, I was jerked back to reality by Cyd's panicked cry of "Snake!" Aware of Australia's many poisonous snakes, I rushed forward as Cyd retreated, almost colliding in a scene from the Keystone Cops, but I couldn't see anything in the path ahead.

"All I saw was a long gray tail," Cyd exclaimed, pointing off in the general direction of Tasmania. "It slid under that bush."

Disappointed that I didn't get a glimpse of the snake, I was now perplexed by which bush she was talking about as well as an alternate route to choose to avoid the snake. Figuring that the snake wanted no part of us either, we noisily proceeded on our original track.

Back in the forest the trails crossed over each other and Cyd and I took turns pretending to know where a particular tangent would take us. We came to rest on an oasis of smooth sedimentary rock amid the bush and drank water from our flask. From one end of the giant gray slab we looked out over the ocean toward Sydney (and New Zealand for all we knew) and lapsed into a dreamy oneness with nature.

Once again Cyd broke the silence with a startling yelp. Sure that it was the adder relentlessly stalking us, I sprang to my feet and looked to Cyd for a clue as to its whereabouts. This time, however, her face conveyed awe, not fear.

"Look!" she said, pointing to a spot in the distance. "Look at that!"

I strained to follow the line of her finger. "What is it?" I asked, turning my head back and forth from her finger to the horizon.

"It's a kangaroo! Can't you see it?"

Although I am somewhat near-sighted and wasn't wearing my glasses, I couldn't imagine not being able to see a kangaroo hopping around in the forest opening right in front of us. I squinted in the general direction Cyd was pointing. "No."

Cyd moved several steps forward and began to trace the outline on the rock face underfoot. "See?" she said, smiling like a child who just found an Easter egg. "It's an Aboriginal carving."

Finally recognizing what she was pointing at, I was stunned. Somehow we had stumbled upon an Aboriginal carving of a kangaroo dating back tens of thousands of years. There were others, too, such as oversized fish and goannas and two-headed snakes. We took care not to step on any of the Dream Time ancestors as we jockeyed for position to interpret the next image. We spent the rest of the afternoon identifying animals and other petroglyphs in the polished rock and debating what the many concentric rings of circles represented.

On the train ride back to Sydney, Cyd took her daily nap while I wrestled with thoughts about how the site we discovered was once home to native Aboriginal clans, and how easy it is for a race of people to disappear with the flick of a snake's tail. In fact, one clan living in the outback near Darwin believes a great snake will be the undoing of mankind if the creature is ever awakened from its sleep deep in Barramundi Gorge. But for now we were content to continue our walkabout of sorts—the real world would be waiting when we got home.

LEAVE THE DRIVING TO US

Although Sydney was friendly and comfortable for a large city, the time had come to seek adventure in the outback and on the Great Barrier Reef. Bus Australia would be our transport (and on many occasions lodging for the night) as we began our plan to explore Australia from the eastern shore to the Red Center and Victorian coastline.

Our route required stopping at inconspicuous little towns like Coffs Harbour and Aerlie Beach and for the occasional kangaroo that bounded onto the highway. We planned to fly across the desert to Darwin, rejoin the bus route through the Red Center and ride back through Melbourne to Sydney. It was an aggressive schedule by most measures, but the spring temperatures, change of scenery and hearty foods had revitalized us, and we wouldn't be denied an opportunity that might not come again for some time.

Taking advantage of the luxury coach, we traveled overnight to Coffs Harbor, a small fishing port protected by an even smaller island that was home to noisy mutton birds and not much else. There we were introduced to the first of many hostels and backpacker establishments we utilized while in Australia. As the Australian dollar was relatively strong against US currency, this was the only way we could afford to stay in country for two months.

Still groggy from a lack of sleep, we climbed down off the bus and were besieged by hostel hawkers, each grabbing an arm and telling us how wonderful and inexpensive their place was. I pulled Cyd aside to clear my head and discuss our options, when I noticed a large man sporting a crew-cut standing back from the crowd, a cigarette protruding from his stubby fingers. He introduced himself as Terry.

Terry was no Mel Gibson, but he had a friendly face that we trusted instantly. He loaded our bags into a plain white van and took us to the Albany Hostel where we caught up on our sleep. "Pay up after you've rested," Terry called, as we climbed the stairs to our room.

The days ahead rolled together into one lazy afternoon of long walks and bike rides around the harbor and bird sanctuary. On Terry's recommendation, we also decided to go horseback riding at a family owned stable in the thickly forested mountains to the west, which from the harbor appeared as hazy, silver dolphins on the horizon.

Cyd was excited about the prospect of horseback riding in a rain forest. I wasn't. The first and very last time I had been on a horse was at a local amusement park back home, where I was led around a riding pen atop a pony more concerned with defecating than carrying its young rider.

The next morning our riding experience started innocently enough as we donned helmets and accompanied the owner as he chose our horses. Cyd, who had some riding experience, was given the steed Trooper, a gallant brown Arabian which snorted contemptuously at me when I walked by. Because of my novice rating, I was assigned to Sunbeam, the gentle tan-and-white mare for beginners.

For several hours our horses walked and cantered through the dense jungle, feeding on stray shoots of grass and occasionally breaking into a trot when spooked by a monitor lizard or long-tailed rat scurrying through the underbrush. For most of the day Sunbeam was the perfect companion. She never broke into a gallop like the other horses or bucked when Trooper bit her. She even took the right path when I accidentally pulled the reins to make her go elsewhere.

I was in total control, admiring surrounding clusters of beech, gum and acacia trees, when our guide, operating on the typically Australian and sexist notion that all men like to ride fast, decided I should try to get Sunbeam to gallop. Neither the horse or I was keen on the idea, and my feeble attempts at kicking and smacking Sunbeam with a switch went unnoticed; unfortunately, the guide's firm slap on Sunbeam's hindquarter didn't. Instantly I was jolted from my uncomplicated daydream world by a horse possessed. Sunbeam sprinted along the narrow forest path, snorting and kicking up dust and practically launching me out of the saddle. I had been on many amusement rides in my life, but nothing could compare to this. I longed for the security of the "pooping pony" from my youth.

Fighting to keep my feet in the stirrups and hold onto the reins, I bounced up and down and left and right in the saddle, while Cyd and the guide laughed maniacally like kookaburras. I dropped my stick and realized that I had lost all control. I was a conductor without a baton. A magician without a wand. A cleanup hitter without a bat. I was doomed.

The wind whistled in my helmet as I tried to right myself and focus on the bouncing path ahead. Sunbeam's sweat and foam soaked my pant legs as each ensuing lunge hit me like a kick in the crotch.

After climbing a steep hill and running off the pain in her rear, Sunbeam finally wore down and slowed to a walk. The others, still trying to muffle their laughter, trotted their steeds up alongside me. "You have to stand in the stirrups like this," the guide said, modeling the technique.

No kidding, I thought, still reeling from the pain emanating from my groin. I looked over at Cyd, who was barely able to conceal her smile. I grinned mockingly and patted my horse. What else could I do?

Later that evening Cyd and I soaked our aching, sore bodies in the hostel sauna. As the widespread pain in my body melted away in the jacuzzi, I replayed my riding escapades for anyone who cared to listen. The others laughed at my disdain for horseback riding, but I said it was nothing more than a subtle form of torture invented by women for men. I vowed never to ride a horse again.

ROOTING FOR THE GOOD GUYS

It was difficult to leave our friends in Coffs Harbour. Even on the morning of our departure, Terry tried to coerce us with bribes of ocean water-skiing and thick, barbecued steaks. But we had allotted only a few days to each stop and had to move on to make the most of our stay in Australia. We boarded the bus and Terry took his familiar position leaning against the lamp post, cigarette in mouth, as the stream of prospective boarders exchanged their seats with us.

Our next destination was the seaside artist colony of Byron Bay, a renowned haven for writers, painters and hippies still stuck in the sixties. Australia has come a long way since its early days as a British penal colony, although the people still exhibit a hardy, often bawdy and raucous zest for life that you'd expect from Captain Cook's children. As the only large nation founded without internal war or revolution, it has prospered under the wings of peace for more than 200 years.

The bus followed the two-lane Bruce Highway along the coast, sandwiched between the Pacific Ocean and the Great Dividing Range, arriving in Byron Bay just after dark. Only a short drive from the Gold Coast and trappings of Brisbane, this eclectic seaside town is a Mecca for budget travelers and sightseers alike. Accommodations at the youth hostels would be tight and somewhat noisy, so we hailed a converted limousine to drive us to a caravan park on the outskirts of town. We settled into our trailer (which resembled an oversized avocado green station wagon) and for the first time had an opportunity to use sleeping bags we had dragged halfway around the world with us.

The night was cool and quiet except for the familiar harmony of crickets and frogs. Other than marsupials, Australia really didn't have much of a variety of indigenous animals, which included reptiles, snakes and some birds. Ironically, it is the imported creatures that are the topic of discussion. Almost to a person the Aussies lament their government's great ecological *faux pas* over their 200-year history. First Captain Cook brought in horses and pigs that today run wild across the sandy terrain, tilling the delicate soil with their hooves and leading to great wind and water erosion. Later, the government experimented with rabbits as a source of food, but soon found out that they, too, destroyed the land by burrowing out of reach. To stem the rabbit explosion, foxes were imported as natural predators and wound up feasting on indigenous mammals and causing greater damage with their tunneling than the rabbits did.

But the most ironic story, and possibly most tragic, is the Florida cane toad debacle. Imported from the United States to help stem the problem of beetles destroying sugar cane crops, the large toad was set loose to eradicate the pesky bug. Unfortunately, and to the dismay of Aussie farmers, the cane toad leads a nocturnal life feeding on various creatures along the ground, while the beetles flourish in the daylight atop the cane stalks far out of reach of the predatory toads. Nature's cruel joke goes one step further, however. The cane toad is now proliferating at such an alarming rate that many of the helpful insects and other frogs it feeds on are near the brink of extinction. The dilemma is literally driving the Aussies nuts and they often swerve their vehicles at the tiny sets of eyes on the roadway or engage in massive toad-hunting expeditions to eliminate the buggers.

Yet Byron Bay is as far away from squashed toads and foxholes as you can get in Australia. A majestic lighthouse, which can be seen from just about anywhere in Byron, stands high atop the distant cliff, a sentinel to Australia's eastern-most point. Our first day's journey took us there to watch the hang-gliders soar at dizzying heights above the breaching dolphins, which outnumbered the few comatose sunbathers at Watego Bay opposite the lighthouse.

The beaches and walkways were eerily quiet and were it not for the chance meeting of a jogger, we might have thought something was amiss. "It's the Aussie Rules finals today," he said, between breaths. "Everyone's in the pubs." Aussie Rules, one of four varieties of football played Down Under, is to Australians what baseball is to us. It's in the hearts and minds of every boy and girl from Perth to Brisbane and all points in between.

Once back in town we walked past the open pubs, patrons three deep at the bar cheering for their respective teams. Cyd browsed the seaside shops while I made my way into Paul Hogan's pub which overlooks the bay. I grabbed a 32-ounce Foster's Lager (which my brother calls the "oil can") and scanned the bar for a place to wait for

Cyd. The back room was crammed with rowdies watching the big screen, so I opted for a standing-room perch near a wall opposite the bar. I had seen Aussie Rules on cable back home a few times and liked its non-stop action and lack of commercials, which plague US football. The wide-open game on the overhead TV was no exception, as Canberra and Sydney matched points and punches in the hard-fought first half.

After refreshing my beer I returned to my station along the wall, only to be greeted by two young Aussies standing in my place. I stood next to them waiting for the second half to start, trying to determine which team they were cheering for. Cyd soon returned from her shopping spree, flashing a smile and a newly purchased cane hat. "What's up?" she asked.

"Not much," I replied, feigning interest in her hat. "It's a great game," I said, still trying to maintain neutrality. Cyd shrugged and went to get a beer, twirling her prized purchase on her hand. The taller Aussie took advantage of the lull in our conversation to speak up.

"Eh mate," he said in a sing-song cadence. "You like Aussie Rules, do ya?"

"Yeah, I've seen it a few times on TV in the states," I answered, taking a drink to reassure him I was a true sportsman.

"Good on ya, then!" he boomed.

Extending a giant hand he introduced himself as Marcus, and oddly, his friend as Marcus, too. Soon Cyd returned to more introductions, and we men commenced to bore her to tears comparing US football and Aussie Rules and cheering the game. From the fringe of our male-bonding, Cyd asked, "Which team are you rooting for?"

"Rooting!" the shorter Marcus shouted.

The taller Marcus spit beer out trying to control his laughter. "What do you mean by rooting?"

Cyd and I looked at each other and shrugged. "I mean, which team do you root for?" Cyd replied.

The Marcus boys doubled over again with laughter. After a few minutes trying to regain his composure, tall

Marcus proceeded to explain that in Australia "rooting" was slang for having sex. Now we were all laughing uncontrollably at the absurdity of *rooting* for a team and how bizarre Cyd's question must have sounded. It was just one of many times we laughed at how different our English was from theirs.

We spent the rest of the evening drinking, laughing, eating Mexican food and comparing notes about world politics, which our two college-aged friends knew quite well. In fact, they knew much more, we both had to admit, than we did about the rest of the world when we were in college.

After dinner they drove us out along the deserted road to the trailer park and chuckled when we showed them where we were staying. We wished them well and told them there was always next year for Sydney, who had given up the fight in the second half and was routed by Canberra.

NUDE IN NOOSA HEADS

We woke at five to the piercing tone of our portable alarm and fought off hangovers to catch the bus in town. Our Bus Australia passes allowed us to debark and, on a day's notice, rejoin the continuous caravan of buses that traveled in a circular fashion around the country. We had purchased our tickets back home and for only $300 would be able to travel for up to six months and theoretically 4,000 miles without backtracking.

After a quick transfer at Brisbane, we passed through towns with odd names such as Nambour and Yandina, Cooroy and Tewantin, and eventually branched off the highway to a place called Noosaville. We had chosen Noosaville because according to my map it split the distance from Byron Bay to Rockhampton, and was far enough north that I figured we'd escape the tourist traps for which the Gold Coast was famous.

We took up residence at the aptly named Bratpackers, known for its health food as much as its lodging, and shared a suite with the first American we'd seen in months. It happened that Mark was on hiatus from his job in Seattle, and had come back to Australia after visiting the Sunshine Coast almost 20 years ago. As he recounted prior visits, we found it hard to believe the countryside could be any less inhabited, but he assured us things had changed considerably since he last visited, and not for the better. Yet he claimed Oz was a magical place and would always remain so (even if only in memory), and for that he was grateful.

After a restful night's sleep, Cyd and I caught the morning van for the beach and Noosa National Park: 1,000 acres of rain forest, wallum heathlands and shrublands which was off limits to the urban development dominating so much of the Sunshine Coast. Shortly after the van dropped us off, we caught sight of several koalas casually nibbling the leaves of large eucalyptus trees just inside the park's entrance. The trail ahead was marked by monitor lizards sunning on trees and hawks flying so near the cliff that we might have reached out and touched them. And to the left and far below, the ocean relentlessly heaved and crashed on the rocks, which spouted spray from eroded portals like great granite whales.

Throughout our travels we had found Australia's national parks hard to beat. Well-maintained trails allowed us to enjoy pristine, natural beauty without being invasive or feeling like one of the endless herds of tourists that flock to scenic destinations such as China's Great Wall or the geysers at Yosemite. Instead, we ate a lunch of veggies and leftover lamb chops from the previous night's dinner at Hell's Gate, a sheer crag formed over the centuries by the onrushing sea. The sands of Alexandria Bay spread out before us like a strip of cotton, tainted only by spots of tanned sun worshippers and the odd umbrella.

We wound our way down the hillside, following switchbacks that never led too far from the crash of the surf. Entering out onto the beach from the bordering grasslands, we were chilled by the refreshing breeze off the curling blue waters and surprised by the realization it was a nude beach. Neither of us are prudish by nature, but we strolled along the waterfront to avoid contact with those tanning *au natural*. It was an odd situation and, in trying not to look, we were more conspicuous that had we openly gawked at the naked bodies.

Keeping our eyes on the breakers and perpetual series of waves, we soon found ourselves face-to- . . . well, let's just say it was our American friend, Mark, swimming in the surf. Attempting to follow the unwritten rule that you don't walk nude beaches with clothes on, we quickened our pace hoping Mark didn't recognize us and the beach bums would understand our dilemma. Unfortunately, our new tack only exacerbated the problem, as we walked into the midst of a group of nudists who could have formed their own colony. Convinced we couldn't beat 'em, we stripped down and joined 'em, frolicking in the chilly surf which had invigorated bathers there for thousands of years. For the next half hour we wore the blue-and-white costume of four-foot waves which intermittently covered us from head to toe. Returning to our body-shaped spots in the sand, we let the hot sun dry us off and warm our chilled, pink skin.

Refreshed and relieved that we hadn't drawn too much attention, we dressed and began the long ascent across Noosa Hill on the Alexandria Bay tracks. Birds and koalas blended in with the thick brush as we moved out of range of the soothing thump and hiss of the surf. Nearing the top of Noosa Hill the forest became unearthly still and quiet except for our footsteps and strained breathing. As we stopped to catch our breath, we heard a loud thrashing in the dried leaves ahead. Thoughts of a wild pig or stray wallaby came to mind as I motioned for Cyd to keep her distance while I checked out the source of the noise.

The crunching leaves and snapping twigs got louder as I neared a thicket in the crook of the crossroads. From behind a bush I saw a raven striking at what looked like a large snake, which was coiling and uncoiling in an effort to scare the bird away. What I saw next made my heart race, for a body attached to the snake turned and hissed at the raven. Backing up I stammered while trying to explain that it wasn't a snake, but a four- or five-foot lizard with a girth the size of a large dog. Cautiously, we peered into the brush were the lizard halted, protecting the egg it had

86

pilfered from the bird's now empty nest. We couldn't see much of anything, but we could hear rustling as the lizard moved in a different direction than our path back to the hostel.

Dinner that evening at the Bratpackers was a mix of octopus and cuttlefish, a ten-armed mollusk left over from the Pleistocene era, which we had seen in the Sydney Aquarium (a point I didn't mention to Cyd until a few days after we'd eaten it). Mark dropped by and regaled us with stories about the Australia of his youth and told us places to visit, never once hinting whether he had seen us in our birthday suits.

The three of us returned to our suite only to find Hans, an eccentric German traveler who always wore black Ray Ban sun glasses, watching television in the dark of the common room. Hans had been staying at Bratpackers for some time and gave no indication he was ever leaving. When he wasn't watching inane television shows, which was most of the day, he was monitoring the short-wave radio that whistled and hummed behind the closed door to his room. Convinced he was a mass-murderer, spy or communist defector, we kept our discussions brief and steered clear of any political talk whenever he was around, as anything we mentioned seemed to elicit a snort from Hans in response.

In addition to the many indigenous people we encountered along the way, we had the fortuitous windfall of meeting other travelers from countries around the world. The list included people from Germany, Denmark, Italy, Ireland, Chile and a host of other nations not on our itinerary. Without planning it, we had also experienced the cultural differences and uniqueness of numerous peoples without ever having been to their countries.

Another piece of good fortune was that from the time we left Sydney we had nothing but clear skies and balmy breezes which gave way to crisp nights ideal for sleeping. The morning of our last day in Noosa was a carbon copy of the perfect weather we'd experienced on the Sunshine Coast. Cyd had been relentless in her efforts to get me to go with her on a boat while traveling, and we agreed that the

Noosa River was a perfect place to do so. An elderly husband-and-wife team at O-Boats rented us a putt-putt for the day and, after learning of Cyd's sailing expertise, shoved a map under my nose and bade us g'day.

I cranked the handle on the engine, which was no larger than a lawn mower's, and pushed off upstream on the orders of Captain Cyd. The putt-putt did exactly what the name suggests, noisily straining against the river's current on its way to sea. While I read points of interest from the map, Cyd managed the tiller and kept us out of harm's way. My monologue included natural facts about the area and I emphasized how the influx of saltwater at this juncture of Noosa Heads invited many creatures such as rays, turtles and sharks to explore the channel. Shielding my eyes from the glare on the water, I looked up from the map and scouted the brackish horizon for circling fins.

Suddenly, my surveillance was interrupted by a scraping sound and vibration coming from under the boat that for a moment brought to mind the gruesome vision of "Jaws." Cyd and I looked over the side and came to the same sickening conclusion: We had strayed too far from the channel and were bottoming out on a sand bar. Without thinking, I jumped onto the sand bar to extricate us from the bottom. Leaving the boat had made it more buoyant and, after wading in the rushing water, I easily pushed us off without damaging the prop or spotting one menacing fin.

Once we passed the marina the ride upriver became more desolate and peaceful as thick mangroves and gum trees replaced expensive yachts and weathered moorings. Lunch was a simple cheese and fruit snack at a small clearing along the shore, close to the red water-skiing buoys which marked the boundary of man's discovery and territorial claim. Further upstream we saw herons and cranes fishing the shallows and an occasional fisherman who waved politely from his tiny boat. The cable ferry crossed quietly behind us, taking cars and locals onto the headland for a late afternoon picnic or romantic stroll along one of Noosa's secluded beaches.

Now we were at the lip of the everglades, the mouth of Lake Cooroida opening wide ready to swallow our tiny craft. I pressed the metal flange of the engine which grounded the spark plug, silencing the putt-putt and the rest of the world, too, it seemed. Holding our breath, we drifted in the reflection of the late afternoon sun as it danced on the surrounding water. We watched silently as a virtual wildlife documentary unfolded all around us. A turtle spun in the rusty water beside the boat. Squirrels gamboled atop trees fringing the lake. A variety of wading birds stepped among reeds and cattails like mechanical men.

Having lived and worked in the city the past 10 years, asphalt and concrete burying my thoughts of nature, I had forgotten how relaxing and tranquil the woods could be. It was so unlike the day-to-day living that I had become accustomed to at home. In a way it was therapeutic. I had to think back to my childhood, long before I moved to the city, to recall experiencing a more peaceful time.

The tide was quickly returning to sea and, with the onset of dusk, thwarted our efforts to venture farther. I grudgingly cranked the engine, bringing the putt-putt to life and sending several of the birds skyward with a start. A giant sand ray somersaulted in the brackish water, exposing its soft white underbelly as it floated downward into the muddy water like a dead leaf in the wind. Now in sync with the current, the putt-putt of the boat's engine accelerated, hurrying us past the empty cable ferry and almost full marina, callously taking us away from unspoiled Noosa.

EARLY TO BED, AERLIE TO RISE

One benefit of utilizing Bus Australia's expansive network was that it allowed us to travel at night, thus extending the number of days we could actually see and do things in Australia. On the other hand, it also meant spending torturous hours rocking and rolling along in a bus among strangers. Yet we often traveled at dusk or dawn, which provided us with colorful landscapes and glimpses of wallabies and kangaroos that weren't as prevalent during the daytime. The 18 grueling hours on the trip to Aerlie Beach was no exception as it offered snapshots of the ocean and wildlife coming alive at the edge of the forest just before dark.

We arrived in Aerlie Beach at 6 a.m. and, as was our practice, sought out the least animated hostel rep, quickly securing a nice efficiency room at the cozy Whitsunday Backpackers which overlooked Aerlie Harbor from atop the hillside. Cyd was nursing a chronic ear infection, so I spent the day buying groceries, washing clothes and doing other chores that didn't go away just because we were traveling.

I walked into town to cash some traveler's checks and, while there, decided to get a haircut. It was here, in an unobtrusive little town on Australia's coast, that I had a hair epiphany. I had listened to people grouse about their hair and hairstyles all my life, and I guess I was no exception. For the first 30 years of my life I wrestled with a mop of thick, wiry hair that to me never looked stylish or presentable. Then, like many men, I began to lose hair to the stress of work and genetic disposition. But in a corner barber shop on the wayward coast of Oz, I received my first buzz cut with the No. 3 attachment. A few swipes with the clipper and five minutes later I had a haircut perfect for traveling.

As I looked in the mirror I remembered crew-cuts I had as a child. I also recalled the bulb-headed beings from comic books I had read and thinking how cool it would be to shave my head. Now, the prospect for me was more real than imagined. My buzz cut looked okay and required little maintenance, and I would probably wear it like this for the rest of my life.

Still feeling good about my newfound hair style, I wandered into a shop advertising sail-and-snorkel cruises to the Whitsunday Islands on a small chalkboard outside. From behind the counter an attractive woman in her fifties explained in a thick German accent that her husband sailed the 60-foot vessel to the islands for a day of snorkeling and beachcombing which included lunch. I ran my fingers across the bristles on my newly sculpted head and peeled off two twenties while the woman neatly wrote my name in the register. I later surprised Cyd with the tickets, but she was too focused on my new hair cut; she liked it.

Early the next morning Cyd and I walked the mile or so to town and out to the harbor, which was a graveyard of rocks and mud usually covered by the tide. By now several other people had joined us and we took turns wading out to the skiff which would deliver us to the *Thelka*, a massive white and silver sailboat adrift on the mint green water of the morning sea.

The captain wore a blue cap and starched white shirt which complemented his neatly trimmed silver beard and hair. His pudgy fingers tapped the railing as the final load of passengers made their way to the ship. He was every stereotypical sea captain I had ever imagined. With a gruff voice that suited his imposing beer-barrel frame, the salty captain welcomed us to what he promised would be a full day of snorkeling and sailing, "if the wind cooperated." He pushed the throttle and turned the bow out toward the shadowy, distant peaks of the Whitsunday Islands.

Our destination was near Langford Reef, a sliver of sandy shoreline displaced from the neighboring islands. It would be ideal for snorkeling and lunch without the company of other tours that typically arrived later in the day. On the horizon we could see some of the fancy estates of Hamilton Island Resort, while the barren atoll of Langford Reef stretched out before us like a welcome mat.

Almost as soon as we dropped anchor, giant bat fish began to spiral their way upward from the depths, seemingly summoned by the underwater drone of the *Thelka's* engine. En masse the bat fish emerged through the unclouded water, first as distorted carnival mirror reflections, then as a school of tire-sized fish, capable of gulping buns and slices of bread in one mouthful. At the captain's behest, one brave passenger jumped in and fed the enormous fish by hand while we watched them jump and flip like circus animals performing for their fare.

Soon we were all on shore, choosing optimal beachfront sites and donning masks and fins for touring the underwater playground. I was the first to go into the

91

unexpectedly cold water and ducked my head beneath the surface to discover the fantastic garden of coral and sponges, clams and fish the captain had promised. A parade of mullet, parrot fish, angelfish and fish neither Cyd or I had seen before glided along in the calm waters, feasting on vibrant coral and never seeming to care about the two large, strange-looking "fish" that floated awkwardly near the surface.

The return trip was smooth sailing as shortly after we left the leeward side of the island, the afternoon wind picked up and escorted us back to Aerlie Beach. Sails bulging with inrushing air, the boat heaved in the line of waves headed for the shore as several mackerel skipped along in our wake. Our captain delighted the crew with tales of adventure in the South Seas and how on one occasion he motored for hundreds of miles without even a whisper of wind, the engine consuming great amounts of petrol and he wondering if he'd ever make it back to his home of these past 20 years.

The sun was hidden behind the Great Range when we arrived at the harbor and disembarked the ship for home. Orange, pink and blue wisps of clouds swirled in the graying sky beyond the marina, blackening the hillside as we walked back to the hostel on wobbly legs. But even as we discussed the prospect of staying in Aerlie Beach, with its cozy harbor and spectacular reefs, the lure of a greater mystery prompted a call to Bus Australia. We made reservations for Cairns the next day and the world's largest underwater playground, the Great Barrier Reef.

A DATE WITH DESTINY

I had to admit I was quite nervous when we arrived late in the evening at Cairns, gateway to the reef and source of my greatest fear, sharks. I was reluctant to tell Cyd about my anxiety, and I tossed and turned all night in anticipation of what the dawn would bring.

The next morning we booked a day-long reef cruise on the Sea Star, which offered resort dives and snorkeling at Michaelmas Caye and Hastings Reef. I could hardly sign the credit voucher because my hands were trembling and clammy. My heart raced as I read about the large fish and sharks we'd see under the watchful supervision of our expert guides. "This will be great," I said half-heartedly.

My problem was that I had always been fascinated by sharks, but afraid too. I can still clearly remember as a boy standing near the viewing window at the Pittsburgh zoo aquarium, watching the sleek lemon sharks glide around and around the marine green tank. I wasn't interested in the lazy nurse sharks that hugged the bottom. No. I wanted to see the ones that struck with the force of a car, with razor teeth and bone-crunching jaws. The man-eaters. Running to the large holding tank, I'd first look over the railing from above and imagine how, or whether, I would get out if I fell in. Then I'd gradually move down alongside the bank of viewing windows framing giant turtles and rays which shared the tank with a family of sharks. I would move from portal to portal hoping to get the best view of the monsters magnified by the thick glass. The pointed snout of a shark would often appear from nowhere, startling me even though I was anticipating its arrival. Then, in a ritual I had performed many times before, I'd put a finger to the glass to see if the shark would blink or snap at my offering with its jagged teeth. No such luck. The rest of the silvery body, arching dorsal fin, silky torso and sharp, pointed tail, would drift by disinterested, following the same circular route it had taken countless times before. I had seen this scenario numerous times, but it still gave me the creeps.

Because I knew how much Cyd loved the water, I ignored my fears and convinced myself to go. Once on board, the two-hour cruise out to sea was filled with snorkeling tips and instructions about protecting the reef, as well as an overview for those attempting a resort dive. Cyd was unhappy she couldn't scuba dive, but the dive master assured her it would be risky due to her ear problems, and that there would be plenty to see and do while snorkeling.

Soon, Michaelmas Caye rose from behind the never-ending undulation of waves, a lone strip of sand in the middle of Aqua Velva waters for as far as the eye could see. All but a 100-yard patch of beach was a bird sanctuary off limits to people. I could only wonder why anyone would venture into the smell and filth generated by the shrieking thousands of molting birds that were in the process of mating or hatching or dying in the enclosed area.

Satisfied that I had secured a section of the reef as my own, I submerged into a wonderland unlike any I'd ever seen. Greater vibrancy than the blue coral of Gili Air. More abundant than any place in the Bahamas or Key West. The coral, rich and alive, provided an infinite kaleidoscope of color in the refracted rays of the sun. A spectrum of brain, fan and antler coral offered sanctuary for fish ranging in size from minnows to mullet which zigzagged as I approached.

Cyd joined me for a finger-wrinkling hour touring the underwater zoo of Michaelmas Caye, swimming far out into the depths that turned gray, then blue, then black as the reef dropped off. En route to the beachhead we saw dead coral skeletons and the muted remains of giant clams whose decay, Charles Darwin had claimed, created the foundation for generations of reef to come.

We climbed aboard the Sea Star for the remaining trip to Hastings Reef. As the skipper jockeyed the boat in the lightly rolling swells, he casually mentioned that we would be seeing reef sharks and other large fish and that we shouldn't grab onto them or put our hands near their mouths. No kidding, I thought. I wasn't sure whether I felt afraid or comforted by the fact that these guys knew sharks were there and still went in the water. I singled out one of the crew and quietly asked, "Do big ones ever come along while you're out here?"

He shrugged and replied, "Sure." His response was casual, as if I'd asked him for the time. "We've seen a few tiger sharks, hammerheads, even a great white."

"Well, what do you do?" I stammered. "I mean, how do you handle it?" I looked overboard and could see mountains of coral and wavering shadows of fish visible along the sandy bottom 30 feet below the surface.

"We get the skiff out and gather everyone up," he said. "No worries, we 'aven't lost anyone yet." I forced a smile.

By now the skipper was tossing bread into the water, enticing schools of fish to skim the surface and piggyback on each other for a stray morsel or mouthful. I had seen this scenario played out with carp on Lake Pymatuning in western Pennsylvania, but somehow the prospect of a food-chain-reaction made this feeding unique.

The water soon cleared as the bread disappeared and a huge, black blur ascended from the bottom. I fumbled for my camera and focused on the skipper, who was hanging gingerly over the ladder with a slice of bread in his hand. The creature I saw in my viewfinder was a fish the size of a recliner. Worse yet, it made a sound like a vacuum cleaner as it sucked the entire piece of bread from the skipper's grasp.

"That's Edgar," the skipper explained while most of us were catching our breath. "He's one of two Maori Wrasses that frequent the reef. The smaller one."

Oh, good, I thought. Not only are there sharks and sea monsters here, but these guys have names for them.

After more instruction and some reassurance from the crew, the group divided into snorkelers and scuba divers. As usual, Cyd was one of the first people into the water, while I followed dutifully behind. Cyd's smile and the tepid water eased my taut muscles, and I began to realize that my fears were real but probably unnecessary. The skipper took the point on our circular tour of the reef, and we joined the other swimmers as a unified wave of arms and legs that I was sure would scare even the largest shark away.

Periodically along the way the skipper would dive down 20 to 30 feet and pull a sea slug or other creature from the bottom for everyone to see and feel. Focusing on one of his deeper dives into the blue fog below, I lost track of Cyd and for a moment panicked. I knew being a strong swimmer Cyd was probably in front of the group, but I looked behind me anyway. Nothing but slower swimmers and the boat bobbing at anchor. I looked back in front, where the skipper's steady windmill stroke cut through the water, but Cyd wasn't there either.

In the excitement my paranoia returned. I tried to control my quickening pulse so as not to attract any sharks. I'd once read in *National Geographic* where sharks can sense distress from a mile away using a sophisticated system of nerves located in their head. I ducked back under the water and caught the shimmer of a white bathing suit almost 50 feet from the group. It was Cyd. She had branched out on her own, swimming in the deep channel between coral mounds while mirroring the slow wriggle of what looked like a large remora.

Now much of what I was thinking and sensing would be unfounded under normal circumstances, and I probably wouldn't have been so paranoid, but thus far our trip had been punctuated by several shark attacks. Two elderly Chinese swimmers were killed by a tiger shark soon after we arrived in Hong Kong, then a great white took a young scuba diver off the coast of Adelaide our first day in Australia. It all made me very nervous.

I began smacking the top of the water to get Cyd's attention, not caring that my splashing was the kind of noise that sharks home in on or that I looked like an idiot to the others. After a few loud splashes I awakened Cyd from her trance and waved her back toward the group, which was now hundreds of yards away. Fortunately, the others had stopped at a section of the reef that barely jutted out of the water, and the skipper was getting ready to feed the fish when we caught up. He pulled some bread and fish heads from a packet in his belt and waved them like a silent dinner bell for the occupants of the reef.

Relieved that I had found Cyd, I was able to turn my attention to the underwater ballet that was about to commence. Within seconds several sea bass, mullet and parrot fish appeared, and the skipper shooed them away in hopes of drawing more fish to the scene. Now, on the outskirts of the group, I saw entire schools of fish moving in our direction, bursting into the sunlit shallows in a cascade of shapes and colors. The fish became larger and brighter, forming an enormous mosaic that soon blocked my view of most everyone and everything. Fish nipped at the hairs on my legs and darted around me in a frenzy to get at the free lunch that was long since gone.

My dreamlike state soon turned to a nightmare, however, when I heard the warbled yelp from a young woman in the back of the pack. "Sh-ark!" I had to lift my head out of the water to be sure that what I heard was what she said. Several other faint shrieks confirmed my fears.

As in every movie and book I'd ever seen, the other fish below disappeared, leaving a void in the path of what looked like two rubbery torpedoes waiting to launch their attack. Somehow they didn't look real. I focused on the sharks, scanning the length of their six-foot shapes, dark gray but for a splash of white atop the dorsal fin. I was mesmerized. Yet the skipper simply swam toward them and welcomed us to do the same.

I found fascination taking over and began to move forward against my will. Convinced that these sharks were used to people or just not hungry, I watched them scuttle along the sandy bottom, dodging rocks and coral outcrops in a game of Pleistocene tag, and felt relatively sure they weren't a threat.

While the rest of the group kept an eye on our primordial escorts, I turned back toward the feeding area just in time to see another large shadowy image rising from the deep. It was Edgar. And this time I was certain he'd come back for some meat to complement his earlier taste of bread. He circled around the group, eyeing us up without turning his massive green and brown head, smacking his bulging lips in anticipation of an errant hand or finger sandwich. But Edgar, while larger than any of our group, turned out to be a shy boy and sank back to the bottom like an unchained anchor.

Soon the sharks were gone, or at least out of sight, and we resumed our snorkeling tour of the reef. We spent a great amount of time inspecting antler coral and spiny urchins while surveying the hue and tint of endless coral beds. It was then that I saw the florescent blue and green innards of a giant clam. Said to be more than 200 years old, these ancient bivalves were the size of washing machines,

97

their insides running a spectrum of purple, blue, green and magenta that resembled a Monet painting.

Cyd floated near the surface as I swam down to touch one of many clams nearby. The sandy, coarse shell provided a solid handhold, which I grabbed like a dentist as I inspected the clam's mouth. The massive pale valve in the center of all that color pulsed gently and I felt compelled to touch it. I opted instead to run my fingers along the velvety purple lip and, to our astonishment, we watched as the clam slowly closed shut. We discovered about a half-dozen more clams of varying pigments and replayed the scenario of opening and closing them with the touch of a hand. Later, while returning to Cairns, the skipper told us that the clams are illegally poached and destroyed for the tasty valves and how he'd seen many clams with holes cut in them, leaving nothing more than carrion for the underwater scavengers.

Everyone had gone back on board and warmed in the sun awhile, and the skipper said we had 15 minutes if anyone wanted to swim some more. Cyd and I jumped at the chance and, along with a few others, had what seemed like the entire ocean as our own private bath. We swam over the reef near the boat and out into a channel which was flanked by two submerged hillsides of coral and sea anemones. There, on the bottom, in the valley between the coral highlands, the two reef sharks lay motionless, resting side-by-side in the drifting current. Then, almost as if they could sense our attention, one of the sharks darted away kicking up clouds of silt in its wake, while the other slowly rose like a helium balloon toward Cyd and me. Recalling the field trips from my childhood, I watched in awe as the shark drew nearer, its features becoming clearer and more menacing. The shark's black, lifeless eyes and devilish smirk seemed to be directed at me, but for some odd reason I wasn't afraid. Nor did I move away. I noticed the perfect curve of its primer gray body and traced the lines of its fins and tail with my mind's finger. Silently, I welcomed my childhood nemesis closer with gently flapping fins and soft strokes as I treaded water only 10 feet above the twisting, shiny shape.

I looked to my left and could see that Cyd was also entranced by the shark's slow dance upward. I'm sure I smiled through the rubber snorkel stemming from my mouth, tasting the bitter salt water that trickled in through the opening in my lips. When I looked back down, the shark was suspended only a few feet below me, so close in fact that I lifted my fins just a bit as not to entice or anger it. Then it was gone. I don't remember in which direction it swam or how fast it disappeared. I only know I didn't see the shark leave, nor did I ever see it again. In retrospect, I believe it was at that very moment when I realized something I'd always known; that when your time is up it doesn't matter how fast you run, how high you jump, how deep you swim . . . but until that day, you can tempt fate all you want.

On the way back to Cairns we laughed and cracked open a few beers to celebrate our magnificent day, and understood fully why it's called the Great Barrier Reef. Cyd and I knew that the things we saw that day were destined to live forever in our collective mind's eye.

TRYING ON CAPE TRIBULATION

After a relaxing evening stroll along the Cairns' esplanade, we turned in early. In the morning we were going to rent a vehicle and explore some of the untamed interior of Queensland. Feeling a bit waterlogged, we had decided to push north toward Cape Tribulation, which by my map was a tiny wart on the thumb-like protrusion of Australia that juts into the Pacific Ocean south of New Guinea.

Up at dawn and on the road before six, it wasn't long before our Land Rover had left the bitumen highway, the city limits of Cairns disappearing behind the Alexandra Range. As we drove along I couldn't help but wonder whether Cape Tribulation would be as Captain Cook first discovered it 200 years ago, a foul place, with jagged, twisting shoreline and mountainous terrain, pounded by savage winds and seas and storms and protected by hidden reefs that could rip out the underbelly of the finest of ships.

The road turned to a scribble of dirt and ruts, and left-side driving made me carsick, yet I was stunned by how rapidly the scenery had changed. The forest on the left had climbed to within an arm's reach of the road, while the ocean to our right occasionally sprayed mist on the windscreen. "Where the rain forest meets the reef" is how one person described it. We pushed on through heavy *bull dust* that coated everything within 50 yards of the road with a fine, beige powder. A young man in Cairns told me they call it bull dust because it's so thick during drought periods that you can't even see a steer standing in the road. "It's also the reason vehicles come equipped with a thick metal bull bar attached to the front bumper," he said, "to keep the animals from doing damage when you hit them."

For miles we coughed and squinted through the wall of dust, eventually stopping for lunch and some fresh air at Mossman Gorge, a boulder-strewn river valley that cuts through the rain forest on its way to sea. As we entered the gorge, it was if we had stepped back in time to an era when Australia was still part of Asia proper and Aborigines were the sole curators of the land now known as Oz. Colorful indigenous birds and bizarre insects crisscrossed our path as we walked in the shade of the forest canopy, a mishmash of giant rhododendrons, strangler figs, umbrella-like fan palms and prehistoric ferns native only to this part of the world and a few dinosaur movies.

This was the largest virgin rain forest in Australia, although it comprised only a fraction of what used to blanket the countryside. What were once vast regions of rain forest and exotic trees had been leveled by logging, development and erosion. In fact, Mossman Gorge was the site of the "*greenies* versus bulldozers" demonstrations of the early 1980s, where local activists tried to block further building of the road and subsequent logging activities in the area.

But confrontation had been a part of Australian history since Captain Cook first chronicled his voyages. While we ate lunch, a snaggle-toothed old prospector told us a story of the early mining days, when settlers came face-to-face with cannibalistic Aborigines in a narrow pass called Hell's

Gate. "The Aborigines tracked the miners," he said, "and waited patiently for armed guards to pass. This allowed them to take their victims from the rear of exploration parties without much resistance." Ironically, he claimed it was the Chinese immigrants, smaller in size than the British, who were put at the end of the line, making them easy targets for Aboriginal attacks. The crude *ocker* even went as far to say that the Aborigines developed a taste for the Chinese. He looked us in the eyes and said: "It might be true, then again, it might not."

I knew Cape Tribulation was only 60 miles north of Cairns, but it might as well have been 60 light years. Beginning on the other side of the Daintree River, which contains seven ecosystems along its winding course to sea, civilization went out with the tide. There were no homes to speak of and only an occasional petrol stop. A few general stores offered supplies, and there was no electricity other than what generators could produce. The lone airport consisted of a solitary red phone booth (which doubled as a control tower) and a grassy landing strip that ran parallel to the road.

The road north had deteriorated significantly since crossing the river, and I was secretly hoping that the drought would continue for just a few more days. We passed several wooden markers which stood as reminders of previous flood levels during what the Aborigines call *Kambar*, or the wet time. In the wet season, the severe ruts and grade of the road, not to mention five feet of water cascading through valleys, make driving almost impossible. But any thoughts of a washout vanished as we broke free of the forest and into a clearing high atop Mt. Thornton. The shoreline retreated back toward Cairns, a snake of green and blue winding its way southward; to the north, pushing far out into the sea, stood Cape Tribulation. Again I thought of Captain Cook, his ship held hostage by Endeavour Reef as the storm raged on, the crew captivated by the mysterious outcropping of rock and forest that formed the cape.

The next few hours were an endurance test for the vehicle and our behinds. Dodging branches and boulders in the road, we traversed the mountains, each turn revealing a postcard scene more picturesque than the previous view. Once the terrain leveled out, I peered through the thick brush that bordered the road and saw a disinterested crocodile sunning itself beside a *billabong* and was reminded that part of the mystique surrounding northern Queensland and Cape Trib comes from tales of saltwater crocodiles (or salties as they're known), and their penchant for devouring tourists. We'd heard stories that varied in length and credibility, but one thing was for certain: the crocs were big and in water everywhere. I'd even seen a photograph of a 15-foot saltie coming ashore on the beach at Cape Trib!

The Australians loved to tell stories, and they were at their best when talking about crocodile adventures, like the local fisherman and famous model who were "taken" by crocs. And almost every Aussie we drank with had a favorite anecdote about a *dill* American tourist who got munched. But one story, which we heard from several sources, stands head and "tail" above the others. This legend speaks of a modern-day Tarzan, loincloth and all, who lives in the wilds near Cape Trib. Sightings have been documented by a handful of people; in particular, two pilots who had crashed and were eventually rescued by the man mountain. Described as seven feet tall and weighing more than 300 pounds, he travels with a pack of dingoes and, unlike the Aborigines, who send their faithful mutts into the water first, he leads the dogs across croc-filled rivers and estuaries.

The story has it that this "Tarzan of the Cape" was swimming across an estuary with the injured pilots, when a saltie took one of the dingoes under. Tossing his human parcels onto the shore, Tarzan swam back to rescue the dog. Dazed and dumb-struck, the pilots looked on as Tarzan snapped the 12-footer's neck and swam the dingo to safety. We figured that the Australian disclaimer also applied here, as what we heard might be true, then again, it might not.

We had been traveling for hours when everything seemed to slow to a hypnotic pace. A tunnel formed by vegetation grew around and above the road. Black palms and giant ferns, some species said to be more than 100-million-years-old, sprung from every turn, accompanying thick brush and pockets of rhododendrons that occasionally gave way to glimpses of azure sea.

It was late afternoon when we arrived at the Jungle Lodge, a series of simple bunkhouses that circle a clearing somewhere in the middle of Cape Tribulation National Park. Oversized plants and wild flowers of various shapes, colors and sizes sprouted from every orifice in the camp. Mt. Sorrow, aptly named by Captain Cook during his travails off the coast, formed a pyramidal backdrop to what would be our jungle home for the next few days.

After check-in and a brief tour, we gathered some maps and headed along the dirt road toward the beach. We made our way through a twisted patch of forest, over some dried-up mangrove swamps and onto a pristine beachhead. From overhead, two sulfur-breasted cockatoos trumpeted our arrival. Coconut trees lined the beach like a parade route as the surf crashed in time with the brush of wind in the palms. In the distance, standing quietly at attention, was Cape Tribulation, unchanged from Cook's time but for weathering of wind and rain and tide. We felt like children at recess and began to run toward the Cape, sprinting over the long shadows of palm trees stretched out like railroad ties along our path. Drawing near the monolith we slowed to a trot, turning slowly in circles as not to miss one bit of this paradise.

The sun hung lazily on the horizon as we began our ascent of Cape Trib; like any mountain, it begged to be climbed. Hand over fist we silently tugged and pulled and muscled our way up the craggy mountain face. Lizards and small rodents scurried from under foot as a lone albatross circled off the point. We pressed on, not sure if we had enough daylight or energy to get to the top.

As we rose above the forest, we saw what had captivated Cook and his crew. The peak of Cape Trib loomed above as all of Australia, and the rest of the world for that matter, seemed to fade away down the coast. A great sea eagle broke the reverent silence, screeching as it soared along the cliff, a dot of silver and white speeding across the aqua blue waves that crashed below.

Now balanced on the tip of Mt. Sorrow, the sun painted a spectrum of colors in the sky from the sea to the horizon, casting an orange afternoon glow on our brown, dusty skin. The jungle chorus was coming to life as birds and insects began to sing their evening songs. All the pressures and concerns we had ever known to that point in our lives were gone, washed away with the surf below, evaporating in the last rays of sunshine. It was then, at a time when I felt most at ease with the world, far away from the world I knew, that I did something I never thought I'd do: I asked Cyd to marry me. She was so surprised that she failed to respond. I must admit, I surprised myself, and when I asked her again she showed her acceptance with tears and a tight hug.

I had always wondered whether I would get married or even meet someone who I thought could put up with me. In fact, most of my life I espoused the "evils" of marriage and the subsequent loss of independence. But as was often the case with Cyd, she proved me wrong. After all, she had given up a promising career, shed the good life and lived out of a backpack all to achieve a dream we shared.

After a few moments of silent reflection, we began our trip back to the lodge. Racing the setting sun, we scurried down the hillside, vowing to return the next morning to climb over the mountaintop and explore the adjacent bay.

That night, as we dined on generous portions of steaks, veggies, beet root and *billy tea*, we heard about a local crony and his son who conducted night tours through the rain forest. While most of the camp partied at the only pub in town, we went in search of other night life. We were gathered up by a titan of a man named Lawrence, who would be our guide for the next two hours as we explored the pitch black rain forest that brought to mind Milton's "darkness visible." Armed with large flashlights and insect repellent that could take rust off a car's bumper, we began our hike to the top of Mt. Sorrow.

Dodging stinging plants, poisonous spiders and vines that dangled at neck level, we hoped to catch a glimpse of weird creatures like the tree kangaroo, which Lawrence said was "out there somewhere." Directing our flashlight beams between the path and strange noises emanating from above the jungle floor, we dutifully followed our guide. As I took up the rear of our party, I couldn't help thinking about the Aborigines' strategy to pick off Chinese from the end of the line. Suddenly, excited shouts from the head of the group refocused my attention.

Lawrence had found a bandicoot, a pudgy llittle critter not unlike the North American opossum. The animal sat quietly in the beam of our spotlights, then wandered harmlessly between Lawrence's legs and back into the forest. The rest of the tour produced similar, yet strangely unique creatures, including long-tailed rats, spiny lizards, miniature snakes and even a feral pig. But the catch of the evening was a seven-foot amethyst python, which Lawrence, who I was beginning to think might be this Tarzan we'd heard about, deftly pulled from a pit where the animal lay sleeping. The shimmering, golden snake coiled sensually around our guide's arm and playfully poked its tail inside his shirt. As I stood by with a lantern so others could take photos, the snake calmly slid around and up my arm, lightly pulsing as it moved. Without warning the python constricted on my wrist, creating a living tourniquet that virtually cut off all feeling to my hand. I held firmly onto the lantern, thinking that the light was somehow my only salvation. Then, before I could utter a whimper, the great snake eased off. Round one, I thought, went to the reptile.

Excited by the capture of a snake, we were primed to do some croc spotting along the estuary. As we dodged exposed roots and humus covering the forest floor, Lawrence recounted how on two separate occasions he had almost been "taken" by a croc. He also told a few jokes about how Americans were the croc's favorite snack food. I didn't mind being the brunt of another country's humor, as long as I got to see an enormous saltie in the wild. What we saw were eyes. Tiny red eyes floating on the water, mirroring our spotlights like safety reflectors on a child's bike. Lawrence assured us that the big ones were out there.

"If you don't believe me," he said, "go for a swim." He didn't get any takers.

Exhausted from our day of discovery, we returned to camp where we spent the night sleeping with what seemed like half the animals in the forest. Long-tailed rats and bandicoots ransacked our cabin, pillaging our supplies in search of toothpaste and other midnight snacks. Like fighter planes, bats darted in through the windows, downed a few mosquitoes and moths, and disappeared without a trace.

We awoke at dawn to the caws and screeches of kites and parrots and the maniacal laugh of a kookaburra that sounded like Woody Woodpecker on acid. A local farmer shared lively banter about the state of the world economy with a morning buffet replete with star fruit, guavas, pineapples and coconuts. Having had our fill of *bush tucker,* we began our journey over the top of Cape Trib. Though it was early in the day, the heat was already stifling, but at least that kept the *mozzies* in check. Unfortunately, it didn't stop the blow flies from swarming our eyes and mouths, or sand fleas from feasting on our exposed extremities as we clung to vines and tree limbs along the cliff.

When we reached the peak we were shocked by how the quickly the mountain outcrop dropped away to the sea several hundred feet below. My thoughts again turned to how Captain Cook must have felt stranded on the reef just off the coast, as he entered the name "Cape Tribulation" in the ship's log. After assessing the situation, we began our descent down the parched mountainside. Reaching the bottom we splashed cool, stinging saltwater on our faces and surveyed the path ahead. We had to choose between the jagged rocks along the shoreline or go back up the cliff to reach the next bay. We chose the low road along the rocks, which immediately paid off in the form of several black petrels gliding within reach above the waves, mirroring the murky outline of a sea turtle drifting just below the water's surface. Within an hour we were wading and washing away dirt and sweat in the crystal-clear water of the adjoining bay.

We were scheduled to fly to Darwin in the morning, so we had to say good-bye to Cape Trib. As we wound along the dusty road back to Cairns, I couldn't help but keep looking back whenever the forest relented. It was as if a part of us were left behind, caught on the reef or cliff, to mark our place in time. Just as Captain Cook and his crew were held captive by the cape, I knew that we could never completely escape its grasp either.

CHAPTER 4 ─────────────────

CHARLES DARWIN MEETS MAD MAX

Anthropologists believe the Aborigines arrived on the Australian continent between 25,000 and 40,000 BC, using what were once land bridges between New Guinea and the Asian mainland. When the sea returned and subsequently ended migration patterns, it also cut off contact with any advancing societies. I had read a lot about these native people, whose land was usurped by settlers; they were suffering many of the same societal pains and injustices as the American Indian. They kept to themselves for the most part, and I had seen only a few in the streets of Sydney and Cairns. Typically they'd huddle in small groups around a shady tree or gazebo, rattling off songlines and cajoling each other in a test of memory and manliness.

To learn more about these people and their ancient culture, we had planned to visit Darwin, a northern seaport that adjoined the only true remaining Aboriginal lands. Darwin would be more than a two-day's drive along 1,200 parched and barren miles of road through the outback, which is indicative of travel Down Under. It's as if a single road skirts the perimeter of the entire continent, bisecting the country right through the heart of the desert. We chose to fly to Darwin instead, saving time and, ultimately, wear and tear on our bodies.

As our DC-9 climbed to cruising altitude, the scattered clouds over Cairns quickly turned into foreboding cumulonimbus formations over the Dividing Range, the last fertile region we'd see for some time. During the flight I paged through *The Songlines*, in which Bruce Chatwin relates spiritual philosophies throughout the ages to his sojourn. I found it fascinating how he linked adages from around the world to the Dreaming Tracks followed by the Aborigines since the beginning of Man. I also recalled what a one-time bush guide turned bus driver had told me about the songlines and Dream Time, how they were fading from Aboriginal lore. He lamented that the end of the songlines, which were capable of guiding a nomadic Aborigine across the entire continent with little more than the clothes on his back, would also mean the end of the Aboriginal race.

The sky was now brown with heavy smoke and the plane's cabin filled with the acrid smell of burning wood. Somewhere down below great fires raged through the brittle brush and parched forests. Whether ignited by a random lightning bolt or set intentionally by Aborigines to curb future widespread burning, fires were a major factor in the harsh seasonal cycle of Australia.

The airport in Darwin was hot and choking with the smoke from burnt wood, and we quickly hailed a cab for our lodging on the outskirts of town. Named after the famed explorer, Darwin is both a scenic town and upscale resort destination, as well as the gateway to Australia's outback. We had booked a three-day excursion with Billy Can Tours before we left Cairns and spent the day prior to our expedition lazing in our hostel's tepid pool under a heavy blanket of humidity.

The hostel owner explained to us that because Darwin was set in the tropics, it experienced only two seasons: hot and dry, and hot and wet. She also said it was a tough place to live. "The people who come to Darwin do so to sort out their lives," she said. "In fact, anyone who lives here more than five years is considered a local." But the residents of Darwin are not like other Australians or anyone else. They seem to be in a constant state of agitation, and during the build-up prior to the wet season they exhibit a peculiar behavior. "It's called *gone tropo*," she explained. "It's when the intense heat and humidity make a person likely to do just about anything." I wondered about her, then left to do some shopping.

As I entered the local grocery I met my first Aborigine, a coal-black man with dark eyes and yellowish teeth that branched in varying directions from his bright pink gums. He smiled politely and turned to another man, continuing a discussion I had interrupted upon opening the door.

"Tom, it's been a long time since we've seen each other," he said to the tanned man in a suit, who was preoccupied with two heads of lettuce, which he balanced in his hands in an effort to judge which was better.

Without turning to acknowledge the Aborigine, the man replied, "Yes. Yes, it has, Joseph," as if he'd played this scenario out before.

As the man pushed his finger into the fleshy skin of a tomato, the Aborigine leaned close and said, "It's been two years, eleven months and three days." He smiled.

The man chuckled and so did I, but the Aborigine just shrugged his shoulders and said, "It has. We met right here."

Carrying a basket of vegetables, the man turned and replied, "Joseph, you're probably right." He then said good-bye and walked to the cash register.

In the wake of the man's footsteps I heard the Aborigine quietly repeat, "Two years, eleven months and three days." And I believed him. After all, a race of people who can sing their way across the deserts and wastelands of this massive island, recalling obscure water holes and shady trees and scant sources of food, can certainly remember a name and time and place. I returned to the hostel with our dinner and told Cyd about the conversation I had overheard. We hoped that his would be the first of many.

After a good night's sleep, we were the last two people picked up by the Daihatsu mini-van that would be our only link with civilization the next few days on the outback tour. Dragging our day pack aboard, we were greeted with sleepy eyes and friendly hellos from the 10 other people in the group. Of course, that was not counting Max, guide, friend of man and lunatic Aussie who would share with us what he called "magic" places and sights in the days ahead. His leathery, dimpled face was large and animated when he spoke, a wide, bright smile often punctuating his sentences. Tucking his black mane under a weathered Mick Dundee hat, Max would later tell us he played rugby, his stocky frame ideal for the position of halfback.

When Max began mumbling into a tiny microphone about where we were going and what the tour entailed, in a thick Aussie accent that made his speech even more difficult to understand, I had my first doubts about the tour. He alternated his attention between driving and narrating, and I wished that somehow I could have remained in Darwin and persuaded a pub owner or hotel manager to tune into the sixth game of the Pirates-Braves playoffs. A phone call to my brother the night before had revealed that the Bucs were leading three games to two and could clinch the title in Pittsburgh with one more win. Actually, seeing the game on television was probably a stretch anyway, as most Australians didn't care much about baseball and the game would be played at 2 a.m. Darwin time.

Shortly after passing the airport outside Darwin, Max said we would be stopping to pick up provisions for the next three days. He stopped at an open-air market and began reading from a list on a crumpled piece of paper. As he called out each item we began gathering enough apples and oranges, potatoes, corn, cantaloupes and star fruit to feed a dozen people. I playfully cradled a dark round watermelon in my hands like a basketball worn smooth on the playgrounds back home and, after almost dropping it, I casually looked to Max for the okay to buy it. He answered with a thundering, "Good on ya, To-ny," pronouncing my name as if it had 10 syllables, and waved for me to put the melon in the van. (Later, when we returned stateside, I tried adopting this exaggerated way of pronouncing my name, but it only prompted people to ask if I had a cold.)

Max encouraged us to take only what we'd eat, and soon we were all back in the van and headed toward the shimmering horizon of the outback, about as far away from a television and baseball as you can get on this planet. I was beginning to like this guy, Max, and the rest of the group as well. There were two ivy-league coeds from the States and their British counterparts, who laughed off Max's reference to them as POMs, or Prisoners of the Motherland. Norm and Trevor were a father and son from Adelaide who had planned this excursion months ago, and they, too, were looking forward to experiencing the "top end," as Darwin was also known. It was Trevor's first visit to Darwin, but for Norm, it was a special pilgrimage: This trip marked the first time in 50 years that he had been to Darwin. The rest of the party comprised three Spaniards who spoke little English and endeared themselves to Cyd by taking siestas every day at 3 o'clock sharp, and two young women from Japan: one a Tokyo hair stylist, the other an office clerk in Hokaido. An older couple from California rounded out the cast of characters, who spanned several continents and generations.

Max was now holding an apple in one hand while pinching the microphone between his finger and thumb on the other, which occasionally jerked the steering wheel as the van drifted off the road. Jamming the half-eaten apple into his mouth, Max grabbed the wheel with both hands and swerved onto the sandy berm. "Lookit the jabiru!" Max mumbled. "Two jabirus!"

At first I thought Max was impersonating Fred Flintstone or something, then I saw the cause of his excitement. There, 100 yards across the road, pecking at bugs and grubs in the marsh, were two majestic yet gangly birds that resembled ostriches. While the birds retreated closer to the forest line, Max passionately told us how the Aborigines often mimic the jabiru in ceremonial dances, hopping on one foot, then the other, and tossing spear grass into the air in a tango of courtship. This spawned other stories about lizard dances and various animal rituals practiced by the native people. Throughout the trip we traded familiar comforts of home for the excitement and novelty of the unknown. I was glad I hadn't stayed behind to watch the ball game after all.

After several hours of rattling and bouncing our way over the baked, clay roads that send feelers into the top end of the New Territories, we entered Kakadu National Park, the untamed site that made Paul Hogan and "Crocodile Dundee" famous. *Gagadju*, as it's known by Aborigines, is a vast series of flood plains and escarpment that acts as an ever-changing drainage basin for the Alligator River Region. The boundaries of the park reach down from the Van Diemen Gulf and abut Arnhem Land, the last bastion of Aboriginal culture in its unspoiled state, accessible only by dirt roads and with approval from the elders.

A quick stop at the entrance to the park brought us face-to-face with the unforgiving sun, dry, acrid air and ever-present flies, which prompted the legendary Aussie salute of one hand constantly swatting at your face. We had heard from everyone how the flies could make you *tropo* in a minute, and judging by the many locals we met, who automatically shooed invisible insects from their faces like a windshield-wiper on intermittent setting, it was true.

Inside the park we drove along dusty roads that Max indicated were impassable, often knee-deep in water during the wet season. Max spent the next bumpy hour fielding questions about the landscape rolling by, Aboriginal culture and crocodiles in the wild.

"What would you do if a crocodile attacked you, Max?" one of the coeds named Wendy asked.

"I don' know," he replied. "I've seen a croc take a bull by the snout and do a death roll." Max made a twirling motion with his arm. "It snapped the poor animal's neck, and took 'im under."

Somebody from the back of the bus said, "I heard you should wedge your arms in its mouth."

Max laughed loudly. "The croc would splinter your arms like match sticks."

"What about going for its eyes?" I asked.

Max lowered his head. "How would you get close enough to gouge its eyes?"

We analyzed and theorized about the croc question, while the escarpment, a sheer, rusty wall to the East, rose high above the woody grasslands. Max explained that during what the Aussies call the "knock 'em down season," or monsoons, thousands of cascades plummet over the escarpment, sending raging torrents through the lowlands, pushing over six-foot spear grass and anything else in its way.

As Max turned onto a makeshift sand road that snaked through a picket of ironwood and paperbark trees, he grasped the answer to our earlier questions about crocodiles. "If I saw a croc swimmin' at me," he explained, "I would dive down into the water. Maybe confuse it."

Not sure whether we had an answer, most of us dismissed the prospect of field-testing Max's technique and focused on the rock outliers that blocked the road ahead. A few minutes later Max pulled off the road, turned off the engine and hopped down from the van. "Welcome to Ubirr," Max said. He stretched and put on his hat, motioning for us to follow.

Ubirr is one of many archaeological and rock art sites within the Kakadu boundaries, with some glyphs dating back more than 40,000 years by scientific accounts. "The Aborigines claim to have been part of the land from the beginning," Max said, "when the Dream Time ancestors in human and animal form created the landscape and all living things." In fact, Max indicated that a large part of Aboriginal culture was derived from legends that explain Man, nature and environmental changes witnessed throughout the generations.

Our group formed a line coursing out from the van into the stifling heat of the afternoon sun, quietly listening while Max primed us for what we were about to see. We rounded the corner of a rock outcropping and stopped in our tracks, mesmerized by the life-sized rock painting standing in our way. An ancient red stick-man holding a spear and bag stood frozen on the fiery orange-and-yellow rock face as he had for the past 20 millennia. Max shooed away flies as he recounted the legend which spoke of doing good and living right, the message of many Aboriginal stories.

We wandered into the maze formed by eroding escarpment, looking from wall to wall at the age-old drawings of various indigenous animals and Dream Time ancestors adorning the rocks like an outdoor art exhibit. Outlines of hands waved from great sandstone easels, as Max explained how ancient Aborigines painted using natural dyes which they sprayed from their mouths. There was the alligator man, goannas and two-headed snakes and creatures we could only hazard a guess about; some where small and beneficent, others large and menacing. We stood and sat and sometimes lay on the ground where generations of Aboriginal children learned lessons and lore about their deep, undeniable roots. I'll never forget the image of me, Cyd and Max lying on our backs underneath a rock overhang, looking at the same stone storyboards that spread the word to wide-eyed Aboriginal children so long ago.

The art trail twisted among the rocks and under lofty crags that made us wonder how somebody managed to create drawings there without the aid of scaffolding or other supports. We climbed a random set of oversized stairs formed by land faults and water erosion, eventually reaching the top of the escarpment plateau, which provided a 360-degree panorama of the receding wetlands and flood plain below. Sweltering winds from the desert drove hordes of flies toward our eyes and mouths, seeking tiny drops of moisture to prolong their tormenting little lives.

Upon leaving we drove for another hour and then unloaded the van for a night's stay at Cooinda, our camp site among ironwood trees and scrub brush in the middle of nowhere. A filling campfire dinner was followed by construction of crude tents and mozzie nets, which we built atop two rows of pallets left there specifically for that purpose. After brushing columns of half-inch leaf ants off the tents and sweeping spiders from inside our individual berths, we giggled ourselves to sleep, still intoxicated with the images of primeval drawings and tipsy from beer and wine we picked up earlier in the day. The last comment I remember before falling asleep was how as children the Brits were told that, if they tunneled straight down, they'd eventually reach Australia, and not China, as I had always been told.

A half moon and hundreds of southern stars casted a dim, milky light on everything outside the campfire's flickering reach. Crickets and birds played backup to Norm's snoring, a staccato duet in the stillness of midnight. From deep beneath my sea of sleep I heard whispering and then louder talk that drew me near the surface of consciousness. As I sat up in the restricting confines of my mesh tent, I heard some of the women questioning noises from the darkness in tones that suggested fright and concern.

Now awake with a rush of adrenaline, I turned toward the noises that had awakened most of the camp. Snorts, grunts and whinnies emanated from the darkness, as invisible animals trampled the brittle grasses and brush. I soon found myself outside my tent, shining a small flashlight in the general direction of the commotion. I couldn't see anything and was only sure the animals were still there by their grunts and whistles, which were now accompanied by what sounded like disgusting, wet farts. Then, as the fog cleared in my mind, I realized they were wild horses and pigs. We listened as the pigs dined on fragile roots, tearing gaping holes in the ground with their tusks and cloven hooves.

Many of the group members were out of their tents and voicing concern about the danger of a stampede or assault on our camp. The animals never ventured any closer and we returned to our tents, drifting back to sleep as the sounds of pigs and horses faded into the black. Camping was never this wild in Pennsylvania, I thought, not even with black bears that could rip open coolers, or igloos, as Aussies call them.

Max was up just before the sun, stoking the fire and rousing us with the smells of coffee, billy tea and charred toast. One by one we marched toward the origin of the smell, following our noses toward breakfast and a new day of discovery. We broke camp early, ready to move on to Barramundi Gorge, so named for a unique species of Australian fish that leads a dual life in fresh and salt waters. Max explained that the barramundi starts out as a male that spawns with older females in the rivers and estuaries, then turns into a female that returns from the sea to spawn with the next generation of males. "How long this has been going on is anyone's guess," Max said, "but I understand barramundi is also good tucker."

We continued driving to the gorge as Max somehow stayed on the worsening road. He swerved and skidded in the chalky sand, negotiating hundreds of termite mounds which served as immense pylons. The van came to rest in an open area that wasn't much different than a dozen others we'd passed previously. Max helped us unload the few things we'd need for the day, including a plastic barrel that would protect our cameras when we were swimming and climbing the rocks, and urged us to quicken our step with promises of seeing the gorge.

I could hear the waterfall long before we left the tree-lined trail and was looking forward to sitting in the cleansing fresh stream which I hoped ran from the base of the falls. As if caught in the morning rush hour traffic, our group ground to a halt as each of us had a personal rendezvous with Barramundi Gorge, an emerald lake in the shape of a pear, the fat end curling out toward the falls and source of its life blood; the stem, as it were, providing a thin entry point for us.

Several of us waded into the limpid pool, watching our feet kick along the sandy bottom until it was deep enough to swim. Norm and Trevor stayed behind to bask in the serenity, while watching our belongings and recalling memories from a common past shared by a 70-year-old father and a son 20 years his junior. The Spaniards swam like darter fish out into the green expanse, livelier than at any time during the trip. They were followed closely by the Yale coeds and Cyd, a fast-swimming trio of mermaids. The Brits took up the rear along with one of the Japanese girls.

From my vantage point floating atop the plastic camera barrel, which had been delegated to me earlier, I could see Max helping make Norm and Trevor comfortable before setting off to join the rest of us. He then gathered up the other Japanese girl, who wasn't much of a swimmer, and gently pushed out into the water. Swimming with the Japanese girl clinging to his shoulders and neck, Max arrived shortly after we landed on the slimy, moss-covered rocks adjacent to the falls. Antonio, the only Spaniard who spoke English, motioned for me to join him as we took turns diving under the thundering cascades, which blinded us with millions of tiny bubbles that exploded under the surface in a soapy mass.

"The real magic starts on top," Max offered, pointing to the cavernous trail winding up and behind the falls. I consider myself a far better climber than swimmer, so I took the lead and hoisted myself up the muddy cliff, using numerous footholds and tree roots that made the precarious climb possible. The middle-aged Californian woman abandoned her less-adventurous boyfriend back on the shore, and huffed and puffed her way to the top, accepting assistance only when the ledge became thinner than her foot. Max took up the rear, lugging the awkward 30-pound barrel to a point on the precipice where he could hand it to me on more secure footing. With everyone on top of the falls, we waved good-bye to our friends on the shore and followed Max among the rocks lining the stream above the falls.

At first the rough-hewn rocks pinched and scraped our bare feet, but soon the surrounding chasms and reflective pools acted as a diversion to the pain. Standing at the edge of a 40-foot cliff that dropped into a bottomless green pool, Max adopted a serious tone while telling us the story of how Barramundi Gorge was formed, a legend he'd been told by Aboriginal friends.

"According to the Dream Time," Max explained, "Barramundi Gorge was formed thousands of years ago by the Rainbow Serpent, a massive snake that came here to sleep." We sat spellbound on the rocks, much like Aboriginal children probably had thousands of years ago. Max continued. "It laid eggs in the ground which formed circular pools, then carved a great abyss and ravine on its slithering course to the lake below, where it now rests." Max added that the Aborigines still respect the Rainbow Serpent today, fearing that if mankind disturbs its sleep, the snake will rise up and destroy everyone and everything.

While we scanned the ocher and black rock walls juxtaposed against the pure green stream, Max casually dropped his hat and plunged into one of the circular pools that legend would have us believe was formed by one of the Rainbow Serpent's eggs. We congregated around the pool's rock perimeter, looking into the fizz-filled water several feet below, but Max was gone.

The water cleared of bubbles and we could hear a faint laugh from the other side of the rocks. Max had swum under the rocks through a cave which led into the main stream. "Just jump in and swim toward the light," Max instructed. "Let the bubbles clear and swim to the light."

I jumped into the cool water and was overwhelmed by a face full of ticklish bubbles that made seeing virtually impossible. Disoriented, I swam straight ahead, conking my head on the smooth, underwater rock face coated with algae. I resurfaced to the group's laughter as they had watched my errant crash into the stone wall. I tried again from the water. The pool was remarkably clear without bubbles, so much so that I could see pebbles on the bottom in a spotlight of sun emanating from the cave opening. With a seemingly inexhaustible supply of oxygen, I casually inspected the cavern walls, touching outgrowths and taking mental photographs of scenes that my camera could not. I was anesthetized by the chill and silence and took my time pulling myself through the few feet of rock cylinder that led to freedom.

I cleared the surface with oxygen to spare and heard the cheers and hoots from the group high atop the rocks. Max and I waited in the water as one by one the group appeared from the cave wearing grins of accomplishment. Almost everyone tried the cave swim, but for the Japanese girls and Cyd, who could not risk getting another ear infection.

Satisfied that he had a group now worthy of experiencing the magic of Barramundi, Max climbed several more rock ledges until he was perched 40 feet above the still, reflective pool. "I know ya like to climb, To-ny," Max called from the edge. "Here's somethin' else you'll like." With that, he dove off the cliff. He hurtled downward toward the water as we looked on, stunned by his daring-do and more so by the length of his flight. In a neat splash Max disappeared into the darkest depths of the pool. It took several seconds for him to resurface, but he did so with a smile and waving hand as if he had just competed in an Olympic diving event.

I was next. Maybe it was because I was the only other guy close to Max in age and mental instability. Or maybe it was due to the Spaniards' laid-back approach to life, but it seemed like I was always next in line during this tour, especially when it required something like jumping off a cliff. I stood there for a few seconds, well aware of the diminishing point of return, and contemplated diving or jumping and the consequences of each. Without another thought I was airborne, streaking toward the water, one hand over my nose and mouth and the other cupping my family jewels.

The thump and smack of my body hitting the water followed me down into the effervescent darkness as if I had plunged into a giant glass of Pepsi. I ascended through the bubbles and dimly lit pool until I could see the rocks high overhead through the pane of water above. When I broke free of the surface, Max and the others were applauding while a silent, stinging sensation crawled up the back of my legs and buttocks. I had landed a bit off balance, causing me to sit out upon impact. This was not an ideal entry position from the 10-meter perch and provided me with a red badge of courage I'd wear on my butt the rest of the day.

Some of the group also jumped; most of them didn't. Max was able to coax the woman from California to jump in and the stronger of the Japanese girls to dive. The last event required him to hold hands with the tiny Japanese girl as they counted down from three and leapt together into a memory she would never forget.

Next, we traversed rock faces and crawled through tight portals that afforded new and more majestic views than just a moment before. Max then promised one more treat: the underwater cave. Max jumped into the froth next to a small waterfall and guided anyone willing to do the same from his vantage point atop some submerged rocks. Most of the group walked down the adjoining boulders; a few jumped in without event.

Because I was carrying the barrel with our cameras, I stood alone at the top of the falls, waiting to hand my thirty-pound parcel to Max below. Cradling the slippery plastic barrel under one arm, I balanced myself on a tiny, jagged ledge along the falls. I dug my toes into the sandstone and leaned forward. The next thing I knew I was falling. All I could focus on was Max's eyes, wide with surprise and fear that I would crash on the hidden rocks at the base of the falls. I bounced once, twice, then again off the rocks behind the falls, scraping my shoulders and lower back. For some reason I held onto the barrel, concerned more with the contents than my well-being as I struggled to remain upright during the fall. As it turned out that may have saved me, for when I hit the water the barrel kept me from submerging more than a foot or so. I bobbed in the splashing cascades as Max tried to steady me and find out if I was okay. Convinced that I was fine, he relieved me of camera duty for a while.

I had also sprained my ankle upon impact, but considered myself lucky and well enough to explore the next cave, which Max blithely pointed out was right under the rock he was standing on. Over the roar and splash of cascades, Max instructed us how to proceed and then dipped beneath the frothing surface to show how it was done, though the bubbles and foam obscured our view from the moment he dove under.

Almost as quickly as he disappeared, Max was back on the surface, smiling and asking for volunteers. Still a bit shaken and nursing my back, I was glad Antonio and Juan and even Katie, a high-school swimming standout, went before me. My turn came after the others emerged excited and chattering away about their "weird" experiences in the cave. I took a deep breath and flipped forward into the churning waters, pulling myself to the bottom with two full strokes and a short scissor-kick, aiming approximately for the underwater target Max had pointed out earlier.

In the green-gray haze beneath the surface, I reached for the lip of the arching rock with both hands. I pulled myself head-first into the rock tunnel and noticed how easily the moss scraped away and caked under my fingernails. Once inside, it was as if a switch were thrown and everything turned black. But for a tiny patch of pale yellow light at the other end of the tube, I was buried alive in an underwater tomb. I couldn't see or hear a thing as the hollow casing blocked out the faint light and muffled the pounding of the falls. I inched my way along belly-up in the dark and within a few seconds was clear of the cave and swimming toward the flicker of roiling water above.

As I came out of the water, I felt very much alive. I also realized Cyd was disappointed at not getting a chance to swim in this unique setting. I tried to console her with promises of more wonders to come. She said she was okay, and I kissed her. It was the first time I realized I was kissing the person I would be spending the rest of my life with. I kissed her again and smiled.

On the way back down the steep trail adjoining the falls, I asked Max if anyone had ever jumped off the plummeting cascades. He grimaced and explained that on a different tour a young woman unexpectedly ran and jumped from the sheer cliffs, thinking it was more of a straight drop than the 10-degree slant that it was. Max winced as he continued with the gory details of how the girl hit the rocks twice on her tumbling fall earthward, landing like a broken doll in the water below.

"Amazingly, she survived," he said. "She suffered two broken legs, a mangled arm and various cuts and bruises." Max added that she had to be floated across the lake, carted more than a half-mile along the bumpy pathway, and driven over choppy roads for two hours to a ranger station before the Flying Doctors could take her back to Darwin for treatment. While we swam across the lake, back toward our starting point, I was glad I hadn't taken a spontaneous plunge from the falls high overhead.

The long drive to Yellow Waters River was filled with our tales of discovery and occasional comments from Max, who pointed out sulfur-crested cockatoos and other colorful birds along the road. The air-conditioning had quit some time ago and the Spaniards took advantage of the sweltering heat to lapse into their siesta. The rest of us wrestled with suffocating heat from keeping the windows closed or choking dust with them open.

Finally arriving at the camp, we unloaded the van near a croc-free river, at least that's what the locals said, and decided to take a dip before dinner. I was the first into the eerily quiet canal. Fringed with exotic trees and vines (and whatever could hide beneath them) the jade river stretched effortlessly into darkness in both directions. In a short time everyone was in the water, swimming and floating and occasionally looking over their shoulders for a croc the locals might have missed. The heat and dirt from the day's activities came off in the river along with our cares. As the sun dipped behind the tree line, a concerto of birds and insects warmed up in the night air.

The water temperature ran the gamut from tepid to refreshingly cool and, recalling a game from my youth, I dove down into the chilled darkness as far as paranoia would allow. Upon returning to the surface, I was abruptly greeted by Wendy's horrified scream. Judging from the startled look on her face and panic in her voice, I was sure she had been snagged by a croc. We looked on in horror as Wendy kicked and splashed and screamed a few more times as the submerged attacker pulled at her from an invisible vantage point. Nobody knew what to say or do and we froze in place while the onslaught continued.

In the eternal seconds that ensued we realized that Wendy wasn't screaming in pain or agony as much as it was surprise, and when Antonio's smiling face broke the surface nearby, everyone laughed and breathed a collective sigh at his ill-timed folly. Everyone but Wendy. She returned the assault with splashes and smacks and expletives that drove Antonio back into the safe confines underwater. He later replayed the same trick on me, although the effect was somewhat lessened by Wendy's earlier performance. But I could see how and why she reacted that way, with paranoia drifting in the current and Antonio's long nails digging into her leg.

Later, the campfire's orange glow complemented a fiery sunset above, as large bats, or flying foxes as they're known in this part of the world, glided silently under massive wings toward a night of insect gorging. We feasted on broiled fish, yams, guacamole and fried bananas for desert, while drinking wine and toasting Wendy's 21st birthday with champagne and tales of drunken escapades past.

In the dark halo just outside the campfire's reach, Norm was telling Cyd about his lifelong dream of returning to Darwin before he died. He had been stationed here during World War II, after Darwin was leveled by Japanese bombings, and he couldn't get over how much things had changed in the four decades since he last visited. Tears welled up in both their eyes as Norm talked about the past and Darwin's changing landscape, as well as planning this trip to get to know his son Trevor better. He shared with Cyd Trevor's concern the night before when the horses and pigs raided our camp and said how much he loved his son and wished he could stick around and keep an eye on him.

Morning came quickly with the crackle of a fresh fire and breakfast smells reminiscent of Sunday mornings back home. We ate, dressed and broke camp, this time preparing for a day of canoeing through Katherine Gorge, a series of 13 ravines separated by rapids which are often unnavigable in the wet.

Two-by-two we boarded our canoes and put in at the ramp adjacent to 17-Mile Creek, while Max assumed the role of third paddle in the canoe with the Japanese girls. Norm, Trevor and the Californian couple opted for a pontoon boat ride in the first gorge as the rest of us departed in a broken line of red fiberglass canoes.

Cyd and I had some trepidation about canoeing, as on one of our first dates we battled the Allegheny River and each other in an attempt to work as a team. Maybe it was our independent nature or different paddling styles, but we struggled in a canoe as in no other part of our relationship.

The gorge opened and closed two or three times at a cluster of rocks which formed the skeletal remains of the dried-up rapids. Portaging among the slippery boulders and shallow pools, we scratched and bruised our ankles and shins, while Cyd and I argued about how to carry the canoe. I complained that Cyd was not holding up her end and grumbling every step of the way. Hoping to elicit more effort from her, I borrowed a line I'd heard Max use on Amanda earlier. "Quit your wingin!" I said. Cyd smiled and immediately dropped her end of the canoe, leaving me alone to carry it over the rocks.

Muttering vulgarities in the peaceful surroundings of the serene gorge, I wondered why I ever decided to go on the trip with her in the first place. And I'm sure she felt the same way about me on many occasions during the trip. We had spent the better part of four months together, never apart from each other for more than two hours. We had had our share of squabbles. Yet it was during the most difficult times, when we were sick, or if someone was trying to take advantage of us, or on the odd moment that the trip lost its luster, that we pulled together. Many times we ended an argument by recalling the pearl of wisdom offered by Cyd's mother the day we left: "Be kind to each other."

The venom was quickly extracted from my tongue as incredible rock formations, such as Indian Head and Australia, a hole in the escarpment that looked like the continent, appeared in the next gorge. Without a word Cyd and I were now back together in one canoe, gently paddling downstream and craning our necks toward the top of the ravine and blue swatch of sky that mirrored the river high above the gorge. We stopped at the swallow caves and listened while Max pointed out mud nests of the Fairy-Martin and Bottle Neck Swallows and told us that the raging waters later in the year would wash the 20-foot ceiling clean. We also stopped and scampered over some blistering hot rocks and sat in the shade of the canyon, while Max explained Aboriginal paintings done by the Djauan Tribe. These had remained vibrant yellow, red and orange despite the harsh floods from thousands of wet seasons.

We moored opposite the cliffs and ate carrots and apples in the shade of the sheer wall behind us. Some of us dove from lower ledges and swam for awhile, when Mad Max decided he'd do his best imitation of the famous heart-stopping leap from "Jedda," a movie where two Aboriginal lovers lept from this bluff because tribal law forbade them to marry. Max had told us how on one prior occasion the force of the 60-foot jump split his feet open as if they had been cut by a knife.

It took several minutes for Max to climb the precipice as we looked on in nervous anticipation. We stared anxiously at the miniature figure outlined against the towering crag now yellow in the mid-day sun. Max then shouted something unintelligible and ran out over the edge, continuing to run in mid-air and waving his arms as if he were a fledgling bird dropped from the nest. I counted to three before Max hit the water with a tremendous thwack, which echoed across the canyon a full second later, sending a plume of white spray 10 feet into the air. Amanda counted another three seconds before Max triumphantly surfaced, tossing back his hair and whooping in delight as we exhaled and clapped in unison. Later, Max would tell us it was his fear of heights that inspired him to take such risks on every outing. I thought he was just plain nuts.

The ride home took us past vast gold quarries and brush fires, and we even drove through a gusting *willy-willy* which almost toppled the van upon impact. We thought we had seen everything, when Max indicated he had one last adventure for those of us willing to get a little dirty. He slowed the van to a walking pace and scanned the endless, barren horizon for a cluster of rocks that somehow were different from all the others. Not to be denied, Max found the cave and instructed us to follow him into the surprisingly hot and humid cavern hidden just below the baked surface of the outback.

Although fresh and clean from showers, everyone scrambled down into the first chamber, kicking up dust and misdirecting flashlight beams which ricocheted off the pink stalagmites and stalactites in an underground laser show. Cyd was somewhat concerned, as she feared close quarters the way I did sharks, and she asked me to stay near her as we moved deeper into the cave and away from the sanctum of the dimly lit first chamber where Norm and Amanda waited. We stooped to pass through several tunnels and turned in circles following our flashlight beams and Max's whispering voice. After crawling through one section, we were more than 100 feet into the belly of the outback, then Max turned us back in the direction of Norm and Amanda's voices.

Soon the soothing music from the van's cassette deck welcomed dusk and then early evening as we headed north toward Darwin and the end of the tour. We said good-bye to the two Brits, who chose to spend the night at Pine Creek and save themselves a few hours on Bus Australia as they traveled to the Red Center (a tactic that Cyd and I envied, as we were going in the same direction but did not know we could avail ourselves of that option). However, because we were staying on the outskirts of town, we had a chance to say good-bye to everyone, wishing them well in their further travels. Max stopped the van outside our lodge and offered us the remaining food, leaving us with a handshake and a hug and a sincere "G'day, mate."

RED CENTER MADNESS

Millions of tourists each year make the migration to Ayers Rock, which is leased to the Australian National Parks system by Aborigines who live and work in the desert. As the largest single-stone monolith in the world, *Uluru*, as it's known to the Aborigines, is considered a religious icon of vital importance to their culture; the rock, which resembles a huge tanker rising from the floor of the desert, is symbolic of Australia's tough, weathered people and timeless existence. Yet like Americans who have never seen the Grand Canyon, most Australians avoid the Red Center with its lethal heat and pestilent flies, choosing instead to live around the green, thriving perimeter of the island-country.

We had traveled by bus for 25 hours straight from Darwin, stopping once for a midnight snack at the truck station near Three Ways and then making a changeover at Alice Springs just after dawn. We were captive for the longest leg of our bus tour, and the tandem drivers did their best to entertain us with stories and videotapes which made the trip more bearable. The highlight of the overnight ride came in the wee morning hours, moonlight reflecting on the desolate salt marshes. As most of us floated in the dreamy world just before dawn, a red kangaroo bounded onto the highway, causing the driver to spike the brakes and dump every sleeping passenger from their seats. From my vantage point in the aisle I could see the large, auburn kangaroo hopping in circles amid the light from the headlamps. The driver shook his head and muttered, "Look at this crazy bugger."

I appreciated the chance to see the stunning six-foot adult up close (even if it was from the floor of a bus) and respected even more that the driver had stopped for it. He could have simply dismissed the animal with the bus's roo bar (a heavy-duty bumper used to protect vehicles in collisions with kangaroos), and continued on as passengers felt nothing more than a slight bump, but he didn't. He displayed a respect and reverence for animals, and people and the land too, that we had experienced with most of the Australians we met.

In direct contrast, almost every other traveler we had talked to previously claimed Ayers Rock and the Olgas, a series of towering, brown camel humps 30 miles to the west, to be a rip-off and nothing more than a tourist trap. Although we discovered that such sites in Australia can be raw and uncompromising, we hedged our bets and scheduled only a quick in-and-out tour at Uluru, which started the afternoon we arrived, watching the sun set on the colossal western wall of Ayers Rock.

The first part of our two-day stopover was to view Saturn and some of the constellations in the southern sky at the Uluru Park observatory. I was disoriented, but only until I realized this part of the world saw a completely different night sky than we could see back home. Cyd and I said goodnight as we parted for our respective gender-specific dorms, sharing a $20-night bunk bed with budget travelers from the world over and watching the clock in anticipation of our 5 a.m. wake-up call. Later, in the still, dark silence of the morning, I tapped lightly at Cyd's door and gathered her up as we headed for the bus and sunrise on Uluru. When we arrived at the base of this ancient Aboriginal monument, the sun was just peeking over the horizon, a bright orange flare signaling the start of another day. Within minutes we were joined by hundreds of other passengers debarking from buses and jockeying for photo opportunities of the graduating sunshine on the age-old memorial. We understood what people meant when they said tourist trap.

The sun was well above the horizon when we joined the line of various nationalities attempting to conquer the 1,200-foot peak of this gigantic rock, which up close was much rougher and pock-marked than it appeared from our other vantage points. The climb gradually became steeper and we were forced to pull ourselves up the facade using the thick chain rail put there specifically for that purpose and to help people hang on when the wind gusted to more than 50 miles per hour.

Along the climb to the top we passed many people stalled beside the pathway, either out of breath or too fearful to climb higher, and smiled apologetically as we continued upward. Three-quarters of the way to the top we rested as caravans of Japanese tourists wearing American sneakers and white gardening gloves to protect their hands formed a giant conga line behind us. Several campers who had stayed out overnight at the base of the rock were already on their descent, wearing the sun's glow and beaming from their early morning accomplishment. We reached the peak almost an hour after leaving the base, basking in the sunshine and gentle wind as the boundless Australian desert sprawled out in every direction. I spread my arms wide toward the horizon, matchbox-sized buses and ant-like people at my feet. Imitating Yul Brynner in "The King and I," I proclaimed all of Australia as mine.

Afterward, while visiting the ranger station, we learned that hundreds of people each year must be rescued from the rock, and an average of one person a month dies while attempting the climb. We also discovered that the Aborigines consider themselves caretakers of the land, mourning injuries and death on Uluru as if the victims were from their own tribe. In fact, they prefer you don't climb the monolith at all (a point that isn't mentioned until *after* you descend). But money talks, even in the desert. And although the native people own Uluru, the National Park Service receives a pretty penny each year from millions of prospective climbers, which is shared with the Aborigines along with pain of Uluru's victims.

SPIRITS OF ADELAIDE

Thirty-six hours in the Red Center was enough time to give us a taste of the desert and man's awkward attempt at taming it. We were heading south on the Stuart Highway flanked by the Musgrave and Everard Ranges, dissecting deserts and the entire continent on our way to the port of Adelaide. After a brief stop at a mining town called Coober Pedy, the world's largest producer of opals, which virtually hides underground at the edge of the Great Victoria Desert, we proceeded to negotiate the remaining stretch of empty road that had escorted us more than 1,000 miles from Darwin.

The landscape became less threatening as we entered the territory of South Australia, easing into a grassy valley between the Flinders and Gawler Ranges. Stopping for breakfast at Port Augusta, balanced at the tip of Spencer Gulf, we eagerly sought out a newspaper to catch up on world events. Here, in the oasis by the sea, where the soft morning sun and clement gulf breeze relieved our aching muscles from the lengthy bus ride, I had what would prove to be one of the most discouraging experiences of the entire trip.

It was on Page 3, Section 2 of a week-old *London Times* that I read the devastating news. Somewhat nauseous and dizzy with disappointment, I found it difficult to focus on any of the words describing how the Pittsburgh Pirates, whom I had rooted for all season and every season since I could hold a bat, had lost the last two games at home without scoring a single run. They had been eliminated from the playoffs for the second straight year by the Atlanta Braves, thus missing another chance at the World Series.

I read and reread the cold-hearted story tucked at the bottom of the crumpled page. It was surreal, like a scene from a Fellini movie; I could almost see the script unfolding: *A wayward American baseball fan is reading about his team's demise, a filler story in a belated European paper.*

Kangaroos and wallabies hop around in the desert background, a boomerang twirls overhead.

Cyd, an avid newcomer to the intoxicating lure of baseball, mourned too. Together, we felt much the way Marcus and Marcus must have felt weeks ago when Sydney lost the title football match. We glumly trudged back to the bus, setting sights on Adelaide and hoping to drown our sorrows in the bounteous hills of Australia's wine country.

The bus entered Adelaide proper from the north, passing through a patchwork of parks and between church spires stabbing the bright blue sky. Cyd and I exited the coach and began the ritual of standing back and waiting for the soft sell from a hostel owner, but I wasn't concentrating on where we would be staying or who we should trust. My mind was still on baseball, more so, on sports in general, and how important a role they can play in one's life, if you let them. From the rattan fights in Lombok to the soccer matches of England, there was no getting away from the fascination people have with the workings of the human body. Run faster. Jump higher. Win. It was universal.

After most of the backpackers had scrambled into vans of hawkers promising free breakfast and central locales, a kindly, older man approached us and said that we would probably like Albert Hall, a two-story mansion built in the late 1800s. He said it was set along the beach in the quiet suburb of Glenelg. "If we needed to get to town," he claimed, "we could take the trolley." Sold on his lodging, it was a half-hour later when we met Mr. Albert's energetic wife, who kept the books, coordinated local sightseeing tours and often cooked dinner for guests. We immediately fell for the renovated Victorian home with its high ceilings, alcoves, ornate trim and understated antique furnishings.

Outside, in the air and on the water, it was spring again in Adelaide. We walked the beaches in the cool of deceptive sunshine, wearing long pants and wind-breakers in anticipation of portending squalls or heavy rains moving ashore. Each morning in Adelaide was different than the previous; one day warm and sunny, the next cool and overcast, so we alternated our plans to complement the weather. We played cards, read books or watched television on days when it rained. When the sun shone, however, we rode bikes or took long walks along the beach and riverwalk, or toured the overflowing botanical gardens hidden among the buildings of downtown.

One afternoon, after a day of trolley riding and a picnic at the botanical gardens, Cyd offered to do some grocery shopping at a market in Glenelg Square. When she returned some time later, she told me her story of a chance encounter with an Aborigine.

Cyd explained that while looking for dinner items, she had noticed that a gaunt Aboriginal man with yellowy eyes was following her, not in a threatening manner, but as if he were inspecting each selection she made. "He seemed to be shaking his head yes or no, as I made my choices," Cyd said. "I tried to mind my own business. Then he said, 'Could you help me out . . . with a small loan?' He looked away when I turned around."

Caught off guard by his solicitation, Cyd claimed that at first she said nothing. Then the man repeated his request. "This time," she said, "he told me he was down on his luck."

Compelled by his story, Cyd had found herself saying "yes" to the man who, possibly in his late thirties or early forties, Cyd couldn't tell, seemed kindly and educated, a lost soul of sorts. Not sure whether he was looking to buy food or liquor, which by law is off limits to Aborigines, Cyd followed him around as he solicitously pointed out and then rejected various items, finally settling on a jar of pickles and loaf of bread, which Cyd readily paid for and helped the man carry out the door. They exchanged "thank yous" and "good-byes" and Cyd returned to the hotel with a bag of groceries and a dilemma to ponder. She replayed the scenario over and over for me, each time questioning the man's intent and her thoughts of helping him get something to eat and dissuading him from drinking.

Turning off the cricket match, which was becoming a painful reminder of our baseball debacle, I tried to be objective and console Cyd by focusing on the good deed she had done. Cyd had heard my theory about charity on many occasions, and I reminded her that giving money to a beggar who chooses to buy alcohol or drugs does not reflect negatively on the donor. In fact, once you give freely, you've done all you can; it's up to the other person to do the right thing. After all, I had found (and this trip reinforced the fact) that you can't be accountable for people who aren't responsible for themselves. That might sound heartless, but there it was.

We said little more while preparing and eating our dinner and, finally, we went to sleep pondering life's inequities and looking forward to a wine tour we had booked for the next day.

Winter had returned overnight as we slept soundly on our first firm mattress in weeks. The morning arrived misty and cold. Harsh winds seeming to blow all the way from the South Pole. It did not bode well for picnicking in the wine country. However, they have a saying in South Australia; "if you don't like the weather, wait a couple of minutes," so we hoped for the best and went anyway.

Our tour guide was a transplanted Greek taxi driver from Aukland, New Zealand, whose wife had packed sandwiches, assorted fruits and cheese to complement our wine tasting tour. After a quick loop around the Grand Prix track (which was being constructed for the upcoming race the following week), the van putted out of town, slowly climbing over the fringe mountains of Adelaide which lead to the Barossa Valley and some of the finest wineries in Australia.

We drove through forests similar to Western Pennsylvania in the spring, sampling inexpensive bottles of wine from the Berrien and Yulanda Chateaus and Seppelts vineyards, and enjoying the clear sunny day that had shot from behind the clouds like a cork from the champagne we drank. High as kites we sang bar ditties and told stupid jokes while our "designated driver" politely interrupted with points of interest or anecdotes of his own, finally depositing us safely back at Albert Hall just in time for supper.

ABOARD THE WAYWARD BUS

On the recommendation of our maternal host at Albert Hall, we chose to deviate from Bus Australia and join the Wayward Bus on its way to Melbourne. The bus derived its name from its seemingly random course over the hills surrounding Adelaide, crossing the muddy Murray River and twisting among the pink and lavender salt flats near Coorong, the site of massive sand dunes and isolated beaches. The next three days would be an up-and-down tour of the Victorian coastline, a winding drive along a solitary road well within view of crashing surf, sand dunes and jagged rocks, which could easily pass for California's Pacific Coast Highway. It promised to be a similar trip to our outback excursion with Max, as we shared a van with New Zealanders, Italians and a couple of German women, but from onset the chemistry here was different, especially in light of our lackadaisical tour guide and two loud Brits struggling to wrest the "ugly" title from pushy American travelers.

One of our first stops was Mt. Gambier, an eerie, blue crater lake set in the mountain chain running the southern coast of the country. Later that day, bracing against the bitter-cold sea winds, we watched in the twilight as thousands of mutton birds descended on Gilles Isle, their home. Sspeeding silhouettes navigated the starry sky in aerobatic patterns until instinct drove the birds to the ground and their burrows. All around us birds squawked and screeched in the dark as they scrambled to find the right entrance to their nests for the night.

The final day of our tour began with light snowfall followed by sheeting rain and surging tides that have for centuries carved out the many landmarks dotting the coast. During the day we visited the Lord Arch and a sandstone version of London Bridge, which had collapsed once, trapping people on the remaining section standing in the sea. Later we reveled in the presence of the 12 Apostles, a cluster of monumental rock obelisks guarding the Victorian shoreline against the raging sea and tide on its way from Antarctica. Before making the final run to Melbourne, we stopped at a farm hostel amidst great timberlands and were treated to scones and tea by a friendly farmer and his wife, who allowed us to feed their lambs and tour the natural garden covering the grounds.

We finally arrived in Melbourne, anxious to escape our traveling tormentors, eat dinner and check in for the night. Melbourne, Cyd and I agreed, was a lot like Pittsburgh too, in that it was overcast almost every day we were there. We took advantage of the inclement weather by hopping from tram to tram on our way to visit the huge Victoria market in the city's northern district. As luck would have it, the National Art Gallery was hosting an exhibit by Toulouse-Latrec, so we spent the rest of the first rainy day inside, marveling at the artwork and buying a few prints for ourselves.

As we had in Hong Kong, Bangkok and other metropolitan stops on our route, we spent only a short time in Melbourne, then were on the road again. It was just a few hours before the lights of Melbourne gave way to twinkling stars and porch lamps of rural homes as we passed through the Snowy Mountains. (Upon our arrival in Oz, the aptly named range south of Sydney had received a foot of snow, requiring us to turn our plans in a counterclockwise direction to avoid winter and, ultimately, make the most of the sun.) At this point it became evident that our trip was more than half-way over; in fact, we had been ignoring this fact for some time. We tried not to think about how close we were to returning to the United States, to the end of fall and onset of winter, and rejoining the society which had raced along for almost half a year without us.

BLUE MOUNTAIN BLUES

We stayed in Sydney long enough to store luggage at the train station and catch the first train to Katoomba, a small, unpretentious resort town high in the eastern Blue Mountains. Our final destination was a youth hostel which would serve as our base for exploring an area that resembled the Grand Canyon covered with millions of trees.

After a hectic bus trip sandwiched between two train segments, it felt good to be out in the cool, refreshing air as we walked down the only main thoroughfare, which eventually led to the majestic overlook and Three Sisters rock formation. Using maps of the area, Cyd and I hiked several short junkets along the base of the Three Sisters, out to Echo Point and Katoomba Falls, watching a spectacular sunset from our resting spot on Witches Leap. It was atop the Three Sisters, however, that we learned of yet another Aboriginal legend that would pull us into the heart of the canyon. We were told the legend by a man resembling Santa Claus, who appeared from nowhere to recount the legend of the Three Sisters:

Aboriginal legend has it that long ago in the Blue Mountains there lived three sisters named Meenhi, Wimlah and Gunnedoo, and their father, Tyawan, who was a witch doctor. They were a happy family, as were all the inhabitants of the mountains. Except for the threat of one creature, the Bunyip, who lived deep in a hole on the hillside, they were free from worry. Tyawan knew where the Bunyip lived and, as he had to pass by there when going into the valley to collect food, he would leave his pretty daughters' high on the cliff behind a rocky wall where they would be safe.

One day when he was searching for food, one of the daughters loosened a boulder which crashed to the valley below. This woke the Bunyip, and he looked up to see what was the source of the noise. He spied the three sisters cowering on the thin ledge and lurched toward them.

In the valley Tyawan heard his daughters' cries for help and looked up to see that the Bunyip had almost reached them. Frantic that the monster would devour his daughters, Tyawan pointed his magic bone at the girls and turned them to stone. They would be safe there until the Bunyip had gone and then Tyawan would return them to their former human state.

The Bunyip was furious at losing a meal and now turned his anger toward Tyawan. As he fled, Tyawan found himself trapped against a rock which he could neither climb nor go around. He quickly turned himself into a lyre bird and flew into a small cave. Everyone was safe for now, but in the transformation to bird Tyawan had dropped his magic bone.

Still furious, the Bunyip returned to his hole. After the Bunyip left, Tyawan flew out of the cave and searched for the magic bone, but he could not find it. He searched and searched and is still searching to this day. The Three Sisters stand silently watching him from their mountain ledge, hoping he will find the bone that will turn them back into Aboriginal girls.

Today, as you stand at Echo Point and look at the Three Sisters, you can still hear Tyawan, the lyre bird, calling his daughters as his search for the lost bone continues.

During our days in Katoomba his words would echo again and again in our minds like the call of lyre birds in the canyon.

The next morning we set out just after dawn to spend the entire day hiking to Ruined Castle, which from our vantage point on Duchess Lookout the day before had appeared to be nothing more than a pile of rocks. We chose to descend into the valley via the Scenic Railway, the world's steepest tram line, which hauls tourists in cars that once carted minerals to the top of the escarpment for Katoomba Coal and Shale Company.

We walked for a while in the dense forest, then the vegetation gradually thinned and opened into an area that looked as if it had been dynamited. The next hour was slow going as we tenuously climbed over the skree and remnants of past landslides beneath Narrow Neck Plateau, which dwarfed everything in its shadow.

Once back in the forest cover dominated by eucalyptus, Blue Mountain Ash and turpentine trees, we sighted several of the legendary lyre birds and marveled at their call-and-response, bringing to mind Tyawan's magic and the tragic fate of his daughters. Making good time on the relatively level path, we were overcome with the fresh air punctuated by sweet fragrances of sassafras, gray gums and rough-barked apple trees. Almost three hours after we began, we found ourselves at the base of a steep embankment littered with boulders and tree stumps, the dungeon of Ruined Castle.

The heat penetrated the treetops and made breathing difficult as Cyd and I struggled toward the sunlit opening at the precipice, dislodging chunks of shale and occasionally falling in the musty dirt of the forest floor. Stopping near the top of the peak to catch our breath and review our progress, Cyd lost her footing and started a landslide which unearthed rocks all around her. I fell and watched helplessly as a pumpkin-sized boulder bounced over Cyd's shoulder and continued on, smashing everything in its path to the bottom of the ravine. Cyd sat there stunned in the dust and rubble, rubbing a deep cut in the palm of her hand as a result of her fall. Before I went to her aid, I listened, mesmerized for what seemed like minutes until the boulder finally rolled to a stop in the valley below.

We bandaged each other's cuts and laughed at our stupidity while climbing the natural stairway to Ruined Castle. Soon our pain and frustration was vanquished in a flood of serenity brought on by the sweeping, 360-degree tableau consisting of plateaus, escarpment and now visible rivers and lakes far beyond the trail head. Immersed in natural wonder, I could understand why the Aborigines passed on the songlines from one generation to the next . . . how tales about ancestors and Dream Time deities became one with the world around them . . . and how that to dismiss such lore and reason would be to question their very existence.

We gingerly scaled a monstrous piece of shale and ate lunch amid the radiant noon sun opposite the aptly named Mt. Solitary. In between bites of apples and cheese, we tried to determine whether the river on the other side of the mountain was indeed Devil's Hole Creek, and wondered what was the name of a distant lake that flowed to the South. We also took turns identifying a cat, emu and other eroded Rorschach glyphs in the encircling escarpment, fitting the rock shapes to our imagination like children do with clouds in the sky.

After filling ourselves with food and water, we chose to climb the highest peak of Ruined Castle, a staggered stack of giant charcoal poker chips defying gravity as it rose 50 feet above the ground. The climb itself was strenuous and, combined with the searing afternoon sun, made for a difficult ascent even among the grandiose surroundings.

We crawled through narrow gaps and constricting holes in the rock pillar, inching our way toward the flat, table-sized rock balanced atop the stack of boulders.

About 10 feet from the top (and more importantly, 40 feet from the bottom), my muscles began to tighten as I pulled myself closer to the hard, smooth surface of the rock wall. Cyd was well on her way to the top, but I became frozen for a few seconds at a time, unable to further negotiate the narrowing path or eroded ledge with its mocking foot- and hand-holds always just out of reach. I couldn't understand my trepidation; I had never had a fear of heights.

After freezing and thawing for several minutes I was able to join Cyd on top, exhausted from the climb and anxiety attacks, but enjoying the reward of panoramic scenery by pivoting on my back side. Still unsure where this chance bout of acrophobia came from, I eventually convinced myself to stand, albeit only for a moment, and take in the expansive environs in one deep breath.

Told the sun sets quickly in the maze of ravines among Katoomba's plateaus, we scurried down the hill past the remains of Cyd's landslide and hurried our pace on the level footing as not to miss the last tram to the top of Katoomba Falls and the road back to the hostel. The chilling grip of night mountain air stung in our nostrils as we hurried along the final steps out of the forest. The stars multiplied quickly overhead as if they were meant to supplant the few street lamps showing the way home.

Once back at the hostel, in full view of the other backpackers, we proudly displayed our bandages, knowing that eventually the wounds would brand us with scars, an insignia of trekking in Katoomba always within reach.

Returning from days of alpine coolness in the Blue Mountains, we soon felt the intense sun and hot winds that signal the approach of summer Down Under. Flies would return en masse along with fire warnings and assorted other nuisances we had avoided by touring in the late winter and spring. On our last night in Australia we treated ourselves to dinner at a fine Italian restaurant followed by dessert in a tiny ice cream parlor amid the noisy pubs, restaurants and theaters of Kings Cross.

Touring Australia as we did proved to be a journey within an even longer journey, yet we barely scratched the surface of this enigmatic, strange land made up of friendly, earthy people who flourish in a sometimes unforgiving but always magical place called Oz.

CHAPTER V —————————

NO, NEW ZEALAND
ISN'T PART OF AUSTRALIA

There's quite a rivalry between Australia and New Zealand, and nothing gets it going like mistaking one for the other, or saying one country is better or more beautiful than the other. Both sides claim it's friendly banter, but if you ever get a chance to watch the New Zealand All Blacks play the Australia Wallabies in a spirited game of rugby, you might think otherwise.

We found the Kiwis to be every bit as hospitable as their rivals to the west, though New Zealand itself was more charming and laid back. Stuck somewhere between the US lifestyles of the fifties and early sixties, this place was more safe and secure than any country we had visited.

Aotearoa, or "long white cloud," is the name the founding Maoris, a handsome race of Polynesian Islander descent, gave to New Zealand when they discovered it nearly 1,000 years ago. Dutch settlers subsequently dubbed the islands *Nieuw Zeeland*, which has lasted since the 1600s and early European reign, although the Maoris (which sounds like dowries) retain an active voice in all aspects of government, education and sports, as well as providing a colorful culture which exists in harmony with the rest of New Zealand's homogeneous population. In fact, we had found the people of New Zealand dealt with various cultures in a more advanced and civilized manner than any country we'd ever been, including our own.

After spending Halloween in Aukland, a tidy harbor city which contains one-third of the country's 3 million people, we set out for the treasures of the South Island. For our month of travel we chose to purchase a used economy car with a buy-back option which would provide flexibility, independence and privacy that tours could not.

While preparing to leave the hostel, we met an atypically healthy looking Brit named Nigel who, because of his quick wit and dry sense of humor, endeared himself to us. We agreed to give him a lift to the South Island. Although Nigel would have been the perfect chauffeur for our left-side driving escapades, I jumped at the opportunity almost as quickly as I had commandeered the *moke* on Macao.

The drive out of Aukland was a bit strange, but I quickly got the knack of driving on the left side after accidentally exiting the roadway at the first round-about we encountered. Soon I felt more at ease and commented on how the round-about (a circular intersection where all cars yield to vehicles approaching from the right) seemed more efficient than stop signs and lights. To Nigel's amusement, Cyd and I cynically agreed it would never work with the drivers back home.

Our constant chatter with Nigel and quick stops at places like Waitomo Caves, renown for its caverns and phosphorescent glow worms, made for easy travel the first few hours out of Aukland. We passed from the highway onto a simple road, possibly the only road, leading through green pastures and farmlands that are home to more than 60 million sheep, New Zealand's cash cow. We bypassed the famous thermal springs of Rotarua, which Cyd and I managed to take advantage of on our return route weeks later, and headed south to Howard's Lodge for the night.

It was somewhere between Waitomo and Tongariro that we got our first taste of New Zealand's wonder, as the inverted cones of two volcanoes suddenly appeared in the distance as if newly formed. The sight before us stopped me and Nigel in mid conversation, enticing us off the road for photographs and quiet introspection. We knew we were experiencing something very special, and that that was just the beginning.

Arriving at the lodge just before dusk, we took a quick ride to the chateau situated at the foot of two massive volcanoes. We hiked to the base of the mountains which were ringed in clouds and buried under tons of late-season snow. Standing in awe of the twin peaks, we vowed to return in the morning and trek across the pass between the slopes. It was here that we now understood what so many people had told us about New Zealand: It truly is one of the most beautiful places on Earth.

TONGARIRO RAINS

The next morning we awoke to the disappointment of cold, gray rains and milky clouds that obscured what had been great sunlit pyramids only yesterday. There would be no hiking across the pass; in fact, we spent much of the day lazing by the fireplace, writing overdue postcards and letters and sharing the newspaper with other inmates of the lodge held captive by the storm.

Weather conditions worsened the next day and, bound by our ferry ticket for passage to the South Island, we resigned ourselves to hike the pass on our return to Aukland. Before turning in, the lodge owner told us the remaining portion of our trip to Wellington and the Inter-island Ferry would require driving only three or fours hours tops. On the day we left for the ferry, Mother Nature had her last laugh as we awoke at 5 a.m. to find the rain had turned to sleet, which rudely slapped our faces while we packed the car for the next leg of our drive.

As I negotiated hairpin curves and passed logging trucks that impeded our progress, Cyd and Nigel said little. Keeping one eye on the road and the other on the clock, which was counting down to our departure time of 11 a.m., I instinctively began to speed up. When we hit 55 mph for the first time, a warning bell began to chime from inside the dashboard, diverting my attention for a moment from the prospect of missing the ferry. The bell was part of the Japanese car's design to deter speeding, and would only cease when I eased off the gas. As a result, I had to balance the speedometer needle between the two red fives on the control panel or risk listening to the agitating jingle the rest of the way to Wellington.

Sensing that we might miss the ferry, which could cost us a day or two delay in the port of Wellington, I shoved a tape into the cassette player, turned up the volume and pushed on the gas pedal. The bell chimed incessantly as the B-52s belted out "Love Shack" and other greatest hits on the bootleg tape we had purchased for a quarter in Bangkok. It went on that way for almost an hour, ringing non-stop until we were within view of the stormy seas of Wellington, still 10 minutes away from the ferry.

Amazed that I hadn't crashed the car on the slick, unfamiliar roads, and even more impressed with the mileage we had covered in such a short period of time, we laughed for the first time as I took up the rear of hundreds of other cars in the queue for the ferry. From a booth in the parking lot, a large man with facial growth motioned for me to roll down my window.

"You missed it," he said indifferently, looking back to the charter he held down against gusting winds. "You're too late."

"What d' you mean, we missed it?" I said. "It's only 10:30."

"Yeah, but you have to be here an hour before the ferry leaves," he answered. "That way we can position you with the other cars." He looked at the docket again as if he were reading from a prepared script.

"Well, what are we supposed to do with *these*?!" I questioned, waving the tickets in the wind-blown salt air.

He glanced up and said a cargo ferry would be sailing at noon. "Maybe the purser will exchange them," he said, and hooked his thumb in the direction of an official-looking building near the entrance to the ferry.

I was stunned and angry and unwilling to listen to Nigel and Cyd who offered conciliatory remarks; I even told Nigel to go ahead and catch a ride on this ferry. But he would have none of it and joined me and Cyd as we exited the warm confines of the car and began to the office in the stinging rain and sea spray.

Just then, a weathered young man, with too much of a tan for this part of the world, approached us and asked if we were going to the South Island. I wanted to say No, we're having a picnic here. Instead, I said "Yes, but we missed the ferry."

"Me too," he replied, extending his hand and introducing himself as Craig. We returned the gesture.

"I couldn't find anyone to drive my other vehicle onto the ferry once we docked," he explained, "so they wouldn't let me on." With that he motioned to the two dirty vintage cars I recognized as Chevys from my youth, and which he later told us came from California. He explained he was in the auto refurbishing business, which for some reason did quite well in New Zealand, and frequently shipped relics like the Chevys from the US.

The rain had let up some as we neared the office, and Craig offered to buy Nigel's ticket if he'd usher the second car during the crossing. As it turned out, Nigel was going to Christchurch, the South Island's largest city, which happened to be Craig's destination too, so he agreed to drive the car all the way there for a couple of bucks. Nigel had been on the road for almost three years and had done odd jobs such as pick fruit and herd cattle, so driving an American-made car was just one more experience for his travel resume.

Once inside, our luck changed too. The booking agent said we could be first in line for the 4 p.m. ferry, which had plenty of space, or take the cargo ship at noon. We chose the cargo ship and settled in for coffee and friendly conversation with Craig and his friend Dave, who had driven the second car to Wellington in anticipation of meeting someone like Nigel to take over the reins.

As we discussed how different the US was from New Zealand, and vice versa, Craig and Dave, who lived in Wellington, jokingly argued about which of New Zealand's islands was the "mainland." Between sips of coffee and bites of conversation, our new friends provided us with a half-dozen scribbled names of people to call on while we were traveling in their country.

Soon we were able to drive onto the ship and within minutes we set sail. The trip across the channel was rough going as 10-foot swells rocked the huge ship, so much so that we staggered like drunks between the tiny cafeteria and the cold, sparsely furnished lounge. It was on one of my staggering forays into the other room that I met two pretty women who had waited with us on the dock, their van one of four passenger vehicles buried deep in the ship's hull with heavy equipment, trucks and train cars. Guessing correctly that they were Kiwis, I sat down to talk with them, hoping to glean more information about what to see and do on the South Island.

I discovered they were headed to Stewart Island, an even more remote place at the barren tip of the South Island, and to my delight they told me of places not to miss like Wanaka, the Abel Tasman Trail and Milford Sound. Like every other Kiwi we met, Jacqui and Stella seemed intent on providing us with names and phone numbers of friends on both islands who would welcome us on their behalf. Yet during our entire stay in New Zealand we didn't take one of them up on the offer. Maybe it was because we wanted privacy, or maybe because we were in this thing alone, or maybe just because it isn't the American way. Whatever the reason, we'd always remember the sincere generosity and kindness of every person we met in New Zealand.

KEAS AND GLACIERS AND FALLS, OH MY!

Soon after we drove off the ferry at Picton and waved good-bye to Nigel and Craig in their gas-guzzling bulge-mobiles, we proceeded on the twisting drive across the Richmond Range toward Nelson, a backpackers' haven nestled in the crook of Tasman Bay. It was from there that we could access the seaside trail named for the early discoveries of Abel Tasman and see for ourselves why it's considered one of the finest hikes in the world.

We finally settled in the town of Motueka, which was close to the Tasman trail head, and pulled into the gravel driveway of the Vineyard Tourist Units. Tracks for a small gauge rail ran parallel to the road, disappearing into mountains that spanned the horizon in both directions. A plump gentleman with white hair sidled down the steps of the ranch-style complex and waved hello. I filled out the register and we talked briefly about places to visit nearby and what the weather had in store.

Later, as Cyd and I unpacked the car, I heard footsteps shuffling in the gravel. "Would you like some milk?" the owner asked.

Confused by the offer and sequence of events I replied, "I don't know." I looked to Cyd for an answer.

Laughing, he responded, "Well, either you do, or you don't. It's only milk."

"Yeah, I guess," I replied. "Thanks."

With that he handed over two pints of milk in glass bottles with foil lids, much like the kind we used to have delivered when I was a kid. And as the old man walked away, chuckling to himself and shaking his head, I was reminded again of how we're conditioned in the United States to be suspect of generosity, to question genuine hospitality that people are capable of exhibiting. I was embarrassed by the thought.

That night we dined on large steaks I'd purchased for only a few dollars at the local carvery, complemented with potatoes and fresh asparagus we'd picked up at a roadside stand. We washed dinner down with pints of milk while watching some television on a 10" black-and-white, then retired for a good night's rest in anticipation of a long hike the next morning.

The dreary, storm-ravaged waters of yesterday had been transformed overnight into an ocean of frosty, lime margaritas sunlit against the salt white peaks of the Tasman Mountains. Now at the entrance to the Abel Tasman Trail, we parked the car in an empty lot and readied our daypack with food, water and other necessities for the long walk ahead. Judging from the trail book we signed upon entering the park, we would have little contact with people on this perfect day for hiking. In New Zealand you must sign in at the trail head, as hikers are lost regularly in remote regions regulated only by the hiker's skill and sense of adventure. We began walking. The trail skirted the tropical coastline, providing glimpses of glistening water and isolated bays. Palm trees sprung up from the perimeter of sandy beaches, as ferns and rhododendrons lined the series of streams and cascades on their way to sea.

We shared lunch with a few gulls at Anchorage Bay and regretfully started back so as to complete the round-trip before nightfall. The same trail we had come in on afforded many different views and wonders on the return trip. A flotilla of red and yellow kayaks sliced through the calm waters as birds chirped happily in the underbrush and trees overhead, and we walked for some time before realizing that the pungent smell we kept noticing was wild oregano. We capped the day off with a leisurely drive up the steep road to the top of Takaka Hill, which dropped into sheer ravines on one side and showcased Farewell Spit at the end of the Tasman Trail on the other.

The next morning we set out early in the rain and, as was often our practice during the trip, we once again argued over who would drive. More importantly we argued about who would be the passenger as we traversed through Buller Gorge, a deep ravine forged by glacial rivers over thousands of years. Neither of us wanted to be subjected to the harrowing views of the left-side passenger during our excursion atop the canyon, which followed a steep, winding road without the luxury of guard rails. Cyd allowed me to take the wheel, but somehow we both still felt uneasy. No matter how many times or how carefully we drove the precarious mountain roads of New Zealand, we never got used to it. Once my perceptual vigilance got the better of me and Cyd, exasperated at my back-seat driving, stopped the car on a blind curve, jumped out, and demanded that I drive. She had a way of making a point.

Back on flat land we stopped to watch dozens of seals lunge in and out of the raging surf frothing up through the blow-holes at Pancake Rocks on the raw western shore. It was interesting to see the territorial nature of the seals, diving in and out of the heaving waves that could crush a person or splinter a boat in seconds. Standing in the icy rain and spray misting off the jagged rocks below, we learned why it was named Cape Foulwind and sought refuge inland at cabins near Lake Ianthe for the night.

It was there, in the damp, grassy side yard of our hunting cabin, lodged in the valley running out from the base of Mt. Cook, that I first met Allen. He was a graying, retired miner staying at the lodge, who reminded me of my long-deceased grandfather. While Cyd prepared dinner inside, I listened as Allen spent the evening recounting past travels and staid jokes, laughing at his one-liners until he choked from the heaviness of coal dust and cigarette smoke in his lungs. Unable or unwilling to stand, Allen shifted from one side to the other, propping his head up with his arm and slurring his speech in a regal manner. "M. . . Mr. Tony," he stammered, "please go into my cabin and get my cigarettes from the night stand, please."

Thinking about my own grandfather (who had died when I was a boy and whose voice I could no longer recall), I trotted across the yard and up the steps to his cabin, while Allen continued a monologue punctuated with laughter and wheezing coughs. Inside, the room was tidy and I found the opened pack of filterless Pall Malls next to an open bottle of whiskey that I guessed probably wouldn't last through the night.

With some reservation I gave the pack of cigarettes to Allen, hoping he wouldn't light up and, instead, tell me more stories about New Zealand and his colorful past. It had been a long time since my grandfather had sat in the grass and told me stories. As Allen continued, I pretended his voice was that of my grandfather's, who often told similar stories about natural wonders and the solitude of nature. I was captivated as if I were that curious child of seven again, and hearing Cyd call me away to supper was like hearing my grandmother. I shook Allen's leathery hand as we said goodnight.

When we arose early the next day, a heavy mist shrouding the mountains and sending shimmering drops off the grass and leaves, Allen was gone, as was his red motorcycle, in search of new stories and fresh faces to tell them to. With the mountain snowcaps always to our left, we drove slowly on the scenic road that cut through the thick, tree-lined shaft toward Lake Matheson, which would be our jumping off point to Westland National Park, home to the Fox and Franz Joseph Glaciers.

The morning drive was a series of fits and starts as we stopped whenever a lake or mountain caught our eye and we had to take a picture or just get out of the car and get a better look. A wooden signpost pointed to a dirt road leading into the forest as the entryway to Franz Joseph Glacier, a slowly retreating field of bluish ice concealing scattered deposits of jade. We hiked more than a mile past waterfalls plummeting from high atop the mountains, watching the glacier grow in size and length with each subsequent turn in the trail. Finally, we stopped at the bottom of the ice floe among the dirty charcoal remains of calving and landslides brought on by the rain.

After inspecting the giant, ageless ice-cube, we returned to our car, where we noticed a large, rather odd-looking bird with a long curved beak and talons. It appeared to be pulling the molding off a van and, upon closer inspection, we could see that there were several other birds preying on the unattended vehicle as well. Slowly and quietly they removed the rubber and plastic molding with surgical precision. "Crazy as a *kea*," was how Max had described anyone who had a few screws loose, a direct allusion to these mischievous and rare arctic parrots. We were told that when overfed by tourists and left with nothing better to do, keas, seduced by brightly colored plastic, often vandalized cars.

The next wooden sign along the road indicated we were near Fox Glacier, the not-so-distant cousin to Franz Joseph. It was much dirtier and receding at a more rapid pace than its relative on Mt. Tasman, as evidenced by signposts marking milestones in its recent life. Every hundred feet or so we passed a wooden post that displayed in white paint a date of the glacier's recession, a tombstone of sorts.

It was raining again when we arrived at the glacier's base, a river of ice milk pouring out from a huge cavern formed by the rushing waters. This ice field looked less ominous and dangerous than Franz Joseph, so I began climbing the muddy path running parallel to the edge of the glacier, hoping to find a place to walk out on. As I climbed the sheer stone steps, Cyd fell out of sight and the glacier took on different hues and shades in the dull light of afternoon. I reached the top winded, my muscles aching, but was rewarded with a view of nearby virgin waterfalls and the pristine upper glacier, resting translucent and untouched but for the fine drizzle that fed the river in its belly.

Far below and out of earshot, Cyd was surprised to see a giant chunk of ancient glacier break off and plummet back to earth with a tremendous crash. She was witnessing tons of fallout scatter on the ground as the face of the glacier changed forever in one second, some of it being carried away in the silvery torrent rushing toward the sea. One day there would be a sign commemorating the glacier's retreat when we were there.

Fatigued and leg-weary, I stumbled the last few steps to the bottom where Cyd greeted me like a long-lost friend. She explained that when the glacier calved (which I hadn't even heard) she became worried that I might have fallen into a crevasse or been injured somehow. I turned and looked at the glacier one last time. I wondered how long this mass of ice had been evolving and altering its appearance, perpetually aging in indiscernible increments like lines in a person's face. I thought how transient life is. How extraordinary it was to stand at the foot of a glacier, which has been withdrawing, pulling back to its life's source for thousands of years. This day, this moment, marked the one and only time in our lives, the only time in the four-billion-year history of the world, that this would happen.

The rain worsened and we made plans to stay the night at a local hotel, hoping to see Lake Matheson, known as Mirror Lake, the next day. That night I concocted a batch of tacos made from ground kangaroo meat, which tasted rather good in comparison to the water buffalo burger Cyd ordered and I subsequently ate in Thailand. There was talk Down Under of utilizing kangaroos to augment the cattle industry, but that thinking would probably face the same resistance as venison had in the US. One thing was for certain: Cyd didn't like it.

It was also in this out-of-the-way place, so far from home and all its trappings, that we got our second dose of awful news from home. The news report said that Magic

Johnson was HIV-positive and would be retiring from basketball. My first response was a selfish one, that would not tolerate the loss of one of my favorite Lakers. Then, strangely, I began to think about the young prostitutes in Bangkok. My mind spun back and forth between reality and the artificial world of sports. I wrestled with the fact that when a public figure becomes ill or dies, we all react with passion, feeling that something must be done immediately to right this injustice. Yet ordinary people had been dying from this terrible disease for more than a decade now.

Cyd was upset too, because I had introduced her to the "Magic" of hoops, along with Bird and Michael. She found it tragic that such a young man, who had everything going for him, could have it all stripped away like an errant pass.

The news was doubly ironic for me because of my love of basketball and the Lakers, but also because I hadn't shot hoops in months. Once, while biking in Darwin, I was tempted to join a group of Aborigines shooting around barefoot on a blistering hot bitumen court, but I didn't. I guess when Cyd and I decided to leave our world behind, that meant everything. And when we did that, trading six months of our lives for a dream, we knew we would also miss out on many things that happened in day-to-day living. People would have babies, people would die. Money would be made and lost. Families and friends could move away or return home in teary embraces. We would never know, nor would we be able to get that chunk of time back. Ever.

For some time, and I don't know how long, we sat there stunned in the aftermath of the saddening news, then reaffirmed with each other that taking this trip was the right choice, because as Ervin Johnson had learned, life is at best tenuous.

On the brighter side of that day, Lake Matheson lived up to its billing as from the northern shore we marveled at the glistening, upside-down reflections of Mts. Cook and Tasman in the water. The inverted peaks were being bombed by millions of raindrops sending ripples down their mirrored mountainsides.

152

Deciding to push on in hopes of better weather, we drove steadily up the foggy mountains adorned with cataracts and thundering streams, then through the Gates of Haast in a persistent rain. Not until we cleared Haast Pass did we see the sun again.

The muddy road soon dried, however, and we enjoyed a leisurely drive between a spindly, sapphire-colored lake and verdant alpine mountains dotted with palm trees and other flourishing plants. We stopped at one of the many signs indicating waterfall or scenic walk which we followed while traveling all over New Zealand, this time curiously seeking the Green Pools. Inside the dense jungle the rainfall continued in delinquent, sporadic drops from the leaves and branches overhead. We chatted quietly until we reached the opening and a hanging bridge which spanned a raging river fueled by the rains and glacial runoff. The sign said one person on the bridge at a time, so Cyd went first to test the waters, carefully walking the lone plank as the unsteady structure swayed under her shifting weight. Safely on the other side, Cyd cajoled me to cross, which I did with some trepidation.

We rejoined the path coinciding with the river bed, which brought us to a pool of icy, clear water that the adjective "green" just didn't do justice; emerald pools was more like it. Shadowy, foot-long trout drifted in the current near a waterfall, feeding and unaware of our presence. We moved down onto the exposed river bed, closer to the deep pool and away from the cover of the forest. The color of the water was indescribably bright teal, more brilliant than anything we'd ever seen. There I recalled another pasttime from my youth, skipping stones. I proceeded to skip the flat, polished river rocks across the smooth aqua plane with a side-arm whipping motion. The conditions were perfect. The stones hopped across the water barely touching the surface as I lost count of the tiny splashes in their wake.

An elderly trio from Australia, overdressed and adorned with cameras, wandered down onto the flat and watched curiously as I continued my assault on the water's surface. Cyd was also reliving her tomboy youth, scouting for perfect skippers and flipping them skillfully across the pool. Soon the older couple and their visiting friend began tossing stones and, after a few pointers from us, they were gleefully counting the number of skips and sending the trout swimming for cover.

Nursing a sore arm and not wishing to further deplete the river bed's rock supply, I dragged Cyd away from the mesmerizing pool and back to the car. On the road only a short while, we cut back through another pass where we were greeted by a massive lake, this time a turquoise expanse of water on our left, which escorted us all the way to Wanaka.

AMAZED BY MOUNTAINS

Much to Cyd's chagrin, I had been repeating the name of our next lodging facility, *"Wa-na-ka Back-pack-a, Wa-na-ka Back-pack-a,"* only to learn upon arrival that it is pronounced won-e-ka. Nonetheless, this hostel, run by two American women, enjoyed the perfect setting of a jewel nestled between majestic snow-capped peaks of Mt. Aspiring National Park and the sparkling expanse of Lake Wanaka. But even with the beauty of this setting, the rigors of travel and traveling together were getting to us. We were sick of wearing the same clothes as we had for months and tired of listening to each other's stories about aches and pains. We wanted to sleep in our own beds and eat familiar foods. For the first time in months, Cyd and I decided to spend most of the day apart: I would climb Mt. Roy and she could visit the few shops of Wanaka.

Cyd drove me out of town, past the towering pines and grazing meadows, and dropped me off at the gate leading into the sloping sheep pasture that doubled as a walking trail. The day was overcast and about 60 degrees as I began the steep ascent using switchbacks intended for the farmer's jeep. Lambing season was just ending so I was accompanied by newborns and their protective mothers for my first hour on the hill, an easy walk that was more like a sightseeing tour than a hike. But soon my thighs and calves ached due to the steep incline and change of altitude, so I alternated between walking forward and backward, which provided expansive views of Lake Wanaka and Mt. Aspiring to the rear.

Back in town Cyd purchased some lamb chops and fresh broccoli, compliments of local farmers, which she thought would make for a welcome dinner for me at the end of a long day of climbing. On her return to the hostel she stumbled upon the Wanaka Maze, a series of hedge rows which promised "hours of fun for kids of all ages." Deciding to try her hand at direction-finding, which to this point of the trip had been nothing more than second-guessing *my* map-reading skills, she paid the money and entered the conundrum.

At about the same time, I was leaving the grassy switchbacks for a rutted dirt road that mercilessly gained in pitch and altitude. The panorama of the Southern Alps (which one published account aptly claimed rivaled the Himalayas) helped me ignore the burning in my legs and lungs as I focused on the boundless mountain ranges branching in every direction.

Down below, Cyd was struggling amidst the high walls and claustrophobic confines of the maze. It was getting colder and she thought about me on the mountain and whether the shorts and wind-breaker I wore would protect me from the elements.

Almost two-and-a-half hours after I began my climb, I reached the radio tower and summit which had mockingly loomed above me for most of the day. The only sounds were shrieking wind and the steady crunch of snow underfoot like smashed corn flakes on a linoleum floor. At no other time in my life, including the day we chose to take the trip, had I experienced such peace and solitude. I was above many of the surrounding mile-high peaks as a steady procession of clouds passed within reach. It then started to snow. In a futile effort to capture the moment, I positioned my camera to take a self-timed picture of me against the alpine backdrop and scrambled down the hill a few steps to simulate my ascent. I couldn't hear the buzz and whir of the shutter over the howling wind, and the worsening snow kept me from seeing the flash. So I stood there for about 20 seconds, figuring that if the camera worked I would have a silent picture capturing the essence of Mt. Roy for everyone else to see.

Memories of Christmas and winters back home came and went with the clouds, and I was torn by the conflict of wanting to return and enjoy the holidays with my family and needing to see more of the world like this. As the snowflakes grew in size and number, I quickly ate my lunch, watching the grandeur of pastoral valleys, rivers and lakes beneath the saw-toothed ridge of the Southern Alps disappear in the snow storm as if they were nothing more than a mirage.

By now Cyd had had enough of the maze. She took one of the escape hatches out and went back to the car, muttering to herself why anyone would want to go through a maze in the first place. She took groceries to the hostel and, after a brief walk past the ducks and docks in the leeward nook of the lake, decided she had better check on my progress.

The trip back down the mountain was made more difficult by the accumulating snow and rain. I fell a couple of times from fatigue and the wet grass, causing the sheep to scurry as I alternately laughed and cursed out loud. I reached the bottom, cold and tired and nursing my left knee, and began walking the six miles back to Wanaka. With each step I was reminded of the marathon in which I first injured my knee, the medal packed away with my other belongings. Yet, just then, and probably for the rest of my life, whenever the first winds of winter blow or I've exercised too strenuously, I'll be reminded of another marathon, the medal for which exists only in my mind.

Cyd drove around the lake, scanning the roadside and occasionally looking up on the mountain as if she might catch a glimpse of my bright green jacket. We met up in a tiny cluster of homes dwarfed by 50-foot pines where Cyd rescued me from the cold and nagging pain in my legs, a portent of soreness to come the next morning.

For possibly the only time during our trip we slept late. I was nursing a sore body and Cyd claimed she needed some rest too. We got our things together in a leisurely manner and then it hit me: I would get to bungy-jump today!

5 - 4 - 3 - 2 - 1 - BUNGY!

I had waited a long time to participate in bungy-jumping. Now, as we wound along the cliff-side drive leading to scenic Arrowtown and the famed Kawarau Bridge, my stomach churned in nervous anticipation as if it were a first date. My hands were cold and clammy and my pulse throbbed in my throat as I grew excited about the prospect of cheating death in this spectacular setting.

Cyd, on the other hand, was immersed in a nagging monologue which had persisted since I first mentioned bungy-jumping to her. She had continuously lambasted my obsession with jumping and claimed that if I was stupid enough to go through with it, she wanted all the money and credit cards, beforehand.

I tried to explain that bungy-jumping was not new, nor was it really dangerous. I had learned it began as a ritual called "land diving" practiced by natives of the Pentecoast Island in the South Pacific. To this day the men tie vines to their ankles and dive out of trees in death-defying feats of manhood. The only difference between this and modern bungy-jumping, I added, was that no one had ever been killed jumping in New Zealand.

My explanations did little to allay her fears and she continued her verbal assault until we pulled into the parking lot at the Kawarau Bridge. What transpired in the few minutes before I was scheduled to jump surprised me more than diving off the bridge itself. As I paid for my spot in line and place in history, examining my certificate and complementary T-shirt, Cyd blurted out that she was going to jump too.

Somehow I knew my jump would not live up to two years fraught with anticipation and imagination that far outdistanced reality. And I was right. My jump was not as much horrifying as it was fun. Yet an even bigger thrill for me was watching Cyd go first, diving from the bridge, a limp tangle of cord trailing her down toward the water, a

157

sight which will always remain etched in my mind. And to hear it told by a convert, by someone who until that very moment denounced it as stupid, made Cyd's jump even more special. Her journal account of what she said was the most exciting few seconds of her life and went something like this:

The longer we stayed in New Zealand, the more I realized that bungy-jumping is as normal to Kiwis as a pick-up game of basketball is to us. It's just something you do. And so I began to convince myself that jumping off the edge of a 150-bridge into the canyon below would be a good way to finally face my fear of dying.

All of Tony's encouragement and statistics about how safe it was didn't make me feel any better that bright, sunny day when we approached the Kawarau Bridge. All I could think was, "Am I nuts, or what?" But before I could blink an eye I had signed a waiver, handed over my valuables and been weighed in so that I would be directed to a cord appropriate for my weight. Sans rings and jewelry that could be jarred loose by the jolt, I was like a criminal making the long, last walk up the stairs to the gallows. Except in this case, the stairs led to the bridge I would soon be jumping off.

I thought when Tony and I got up there we would have a chance to think things over, maybe rationalize a way out. But as soon as we reached the top, two men sporting punk haircuts and reflective sunglasses said, "Who's the next victim?"

I said, "If I don't go first, I won't go." So Tony gently pushed me toward the two men. They immediately sat me down and wrapped a thick towel around my ankles before strapping on a nylon wrap, the carabiner and finally the bungy cord.

I was full of questions to calm my nerves. "Has anyone ever died here before?" I said.

"No."

"Has anyone ever been paralyzed?"

"No."

"How many jumps before you retire this cord?"

Smiling, one of the men replied, "We're retiring this one right after you jump."

I didn't ask many more questions while they were preparing me. For the first time I began to hear the music blasting from a boom box on the bridge and the thunder of water coursing through the canyon far below. I also noticed a set of florescent orange footprints which led from where I sat, out to the edge of the landing and then disappeared . . . like I was about to do.

One last check of my rigging and I was ready. The men stood me up, led me on a short bunny-hop to the edge of the bridge and told me not to look down.

"Jump when we count down to one," the larger of the two men said, and then everyone on the bridge, everyone around me, in fact, began to chant in unison: Five, four, three, two, one, BUNGY! With this I was airborne, hurtling face-first at the rushing river, which rippled like a chartreuse satin ribbon that might possibly break my fall if the cord unexpectedly snapped.

After regaining my breath, which was sucked out of me as if I were on a roller coaster ride, I began to panic. I thought I was actually going to die. The sound of wind around me became deafening, the canyon walls a blur, and suddenly the water below came rushing up at me as if I was adjusting a zoom lens. Miraculously, the cord caught and I bounced from inches above the water back up about 100 feet, and then back down again in yo-yo like fashion. I bounced four or five more times from varying heights, finally coming to rest in a hanging inverted position about 10 feet above the water. A large Maori in a raft tethered to the rocks asked me my name and held out a long pole as he gave instructions for guiding me into the raft.

It was quite an exhilarating experience, but as I look back on it, I'd have to say I wouldn't do it again. I thought bungy-jumping was extraordinary, not because of the sport, but because I had faced my fear of death and conquered it. Even if only for three seconds.

THE SIGHTS OF MILFORD SOUND

We drove to the lake shore town of Te Anau in a cloak of mist and rain which we had become accustomed to and checked in to the hostel in preparation for our trek on the famous Milford Track. The irony of Fjordland was that the lush mountainsides striped with towering waterfalls are produced by year-round rains and heavy snow which often make hiking and sightseeing nearly impossible. Heavy rain and the forecast of snow delayed any hikes we might take and we quickly made alternative plans for a boating tour of Milford Sound. Though the Queen Elizabeth II once graced the tiny port in the sound, we would be fishing the icy waters aboard a boat carrying no more than 20 passengers.

The drive from Te Anau climbed through the Stuart Mountains, home to the Milford Track, and descended through Homer Tunnel, which emptied out into the port at Milford Sound. Fog, rain and high winds dampened the prospect of fishing, so we traded our tickets to join a sightseeing cruise along with hundreds of other tourists hoping to enjoy the natural wonder from the sanctity of the ship's accommodating cabin.

Any disappointment we had with the package tour arrangement was quickly overshadowed by the appearance of a mile-high rock formation called Mitre Peak and numerous waterfalls cascading from thousands of feet above the glassy sea. Time and space became frozen as the huge ship sliced through the frigid blue waters on the fjord. We marveled at the verdant canyon walls carved out by glacial movement thousands of years ago, now reduced only to a field of snow atop Mt. Pembroke.

The Lion and The Elephant, two towering rock and ice skyscrapers, rose from the sea to stand guard over the sound. Great hanging valleys spawned cascades and, as the rain continued to feed mountain streams, the fjord came alive with crashing waves and thundering waterfalls on all sides.

As we neared the Tasman Sea and the entrance to Milford Sound, the indigo waves rocked the boat like a toy, and for a moment I was glad we had foregone the fishing trip. Standing on deck, the high winds and crashing surf chilling me to the bone, I looked out into the stinging rain and wondered what it was like to be outside the sound, which was obscured by Dale Point, the same natural roadblock that kept Captain Cook from ever finding safe harbor here.

The ship pitched as the captain turned downwind and back into the calmness of the sound, and I rejoined Cyd and the tourists inside to warm up. Time and time again during this trip, Cyd and I had managed to turn imminent disappointment into delight, which was the case as we laughed and huddled for warmth amongst the elder tourists on board. One of the cabin stewards asked where we were from and, upon telling him of our travels, he loaded us down with candy bars and wished us good luck. This started an avalanche of questions and cajoling from the other passengers. They bombarded us with questions about our travels, vicariously sharing in our experiences and reminding us that you never grow too old for discovery.

Then a garbled voice came over the intercom announcing our arrival at Stirling Falls, a 400-foot cataract pouring over the lip of the Palisades, another towering precipice. Because of the water depth and sheer drop of the mountains, the captain was able to pull the ship to within a foot of the cliffs and, to the delight of several tourists on board, I coerced Cyd and a couple of other backpackers to join me in an icy shower underneath the pelting falls. The crush of water hammered the deck and drowned out our chilled laughter and mixed cries of shock as the glacial runoff stung right through our clothing.

By the time we returned to the dock an hour later, it had begun to snow. We changed out of our soaking clothes and joined the caravan of cars crawling up the roadway toward Homer Tunnel, the only way out. We sat for some time as road crews plowed the snow and spread sand, eventually allowing us to make our way out of the sound. Returning to the hostel we discovered that in addition to the Milford Track being closed, there had been an avalanche which blocked the very same tunnel we had used only hours ago, trapping everyone on the other side for another night's stay.

In the rain and snow of Te Anau we waited another day in hopes that the weather would turn in our favor; it didn't. In fact, the rangers were not allowing any more hikers on the Milford Track until they could be relatively certain there wouldn't be squalls or avalanches. The weather forecast was for more of the same, so in the morning we left with our memories of Milford in the rain and headed north in search of Mt. Cook, New Zealand's highest peak. Maoris call it *Aorangi*, the cloud piercer.

AVALANCHES ON MT. COOK

New Zealand is such a small country with an even smaller network of roadways that it's easy to make a leisurely drive from one end of either island to the other in a day. We followed the Remarkables Mountain Range, a line of gigantic Hershey's Kisses encasing Queenstown, and made good time in the fertile valleys running through the heart of the southern island.

Stopping for gas in an inconspicuous crossroads town called Omarama, we met a retired engineer who refurbished cars as a sideline to running a service station. What should have been a five-minute pit stop turned into an hour of storytelling and reminiscing as "Mr. Blackie" talked about hunting deer with some of the characters he knew around town, and the recent unexpected death of his wife. Then, much in the shy manner of the flute carver in Bali, he led us to the back of his garage where he kept several Model-A and Model-T Fords. "I hand paint 'em," he said. "It's the only way to make them authentic." With that he retrieved an old faded map of the United States from the glove box of the Model-T. Tears filled his eyes as he traced the exact route he and his wife would have taken across the United States if she had lived long enough to see his retirement.

It was a sad reminder that my grandfather too had never got to take the trip he planned for retirement, an ironic twist of fate that befalls many people. Hearing Mr. Blackie lament not doing what he wanted, when he wanted, only reaffirmed that no matter what our lives would be like when we returned, no matter where we lived or how much money we made, Cyd and I would have no regrets about taking this trip.

While Blackie and Cyd chatted idly, discussing the changes in New Zealand over the years, I excused myself to call ahead for reservations at a lodge on Mt. Cook. The proprietor said that heavy snows were making it difficult

162

to get in and that I should make other plans for the night. Returning to the garage, I repeated what the man had told me. Blackie nodded approvingly. "You can stay at Lake Tekapo," he offered. "Nice walks there, and it's close by Mt. Cook. I used to hunt there," he added.

We told Blackie that if he ever decided to come to America and follow the route he had planned, we would gladly put him up for a night or so, and we would have. He was just one of the many people we met in New Zealand, and other countries, for that matter, who welcomed us into their hearts and homes.

He waved good-bye to us and on our way out of town we picked up two hitchhikers (a safe and common practice in New Zealand), who Blackie indicated had been waiting for hours in the blustery afternoon air. The woman, noticeably older than her companion, told us about her harrowing experience bungy-jumping off Skipper's Canyon bridge. She tried to describe what it was like, but her point was more readily made when the young man with her said he wouldn't do it. We didn't mention our jumps and downplayed the importance of such a feat. We deposited them at a friend's house (undoubtedly someone's referral) in the cluster of buildings that form the town of Twizel, and drove along lakes bluer than the sky the rest of the way to Tekapo.

Checking into a neat, fully equipped cabin with the aquamarine waters of Lake Tekapo virtually in our front yard, we ate a dinner of home-made pasta for the first time since we left Hong Kong. We watched television on one of New Zealand's three stations, dozing off in our sleeping bags which protected us from the still, wintry night outside.

In the morning, frost covered the windows of the car and cabin as we sat watching the sun rise over the lake. After breakfast, which for most of our travels entailed eating toast and tea that we carried with us, we drove a few miles to the junction of the road where we could see Mt. Cook, unobstructed by clouds or rain. We drove toward this unmistakable landmark, visible from almost anywhere along the route.

Once there, the sun was blinding as we ventured on several short hikes along the base of Mt. Cook, which presided over other smaller, yet no less impressive, masses of snow and rock and ice. On more than one occasion our attention was drawn upward as great chunks of the mountain gave way and hurtled downward with a rumble and rush of wind, causing us to hesitate and wonder whether we were in harm's way, and leaving us breathless at the raw, untamed power we had just witnessed.

We topped the day off with a brisk walk around the pine forest peak of Mt. Hay, high above the blue lakes of Tekapo as the onrush of wind returned for its afternoon exercise. Because our return ticket required crossing the channel to the North Island in four days, we made plans for a brief side-trip to Akaroa, a quaint French fishing port outside Christchurch in the east, and then cross over to Greymouth in hopes of staying a night at the Blackball Hilton.

THE BAR, THE BIRD AND THE BLACKBALL HILTON

There are queer and wondrous things too numerous to mention about New Zealand, but it's the inconspicuous nature of life on these sibling islands that might have led to calling the inhabitants Kiwis, an undeserving moniker derived from the ungainly, flightless bird native to the country. The undisturbed natural wonder and wilderness speak for themselves in a land where you can drive for miles without seeing another car, house or person. But it wasn't until we checked into the Blackball Hilton, located in the center of the South Island, that we really understood what made the country so unique and its people so proud of it.

Once a thriving gold-mining town, Blackball was a cluster of modest block houses, simple in design and color, with a corner store and pub and, of course, the Blackball Hilton. The renovated pub and hotel with its falsely grandiose name had seen its share of rugby types, thugs, strikers and miners, all at a time when Blackball was a jewel in a relatively unsettled land.

We opened the large wooden doors and entered a long hallway, hoping to find someone who could put us up for the night. The owner greeted us and said that we had our choice of rooms, all of them in fact. It appeared we would be the only guests at the Blackball Hilton that night.

With only an hour until nightfall, we stowed our gear and, at the recommendation of our host, headed out to the edge of town and the cemetery. In the last rays of dusk, we wandered among ornate tombstones commemorating names from Blackball's heyday, the same names we'd seen penciled in on faded photos in the hotel's lobby. Walking back the lone road that runs the length of Blackball, dodging stray dogs and surveying the houses for a glimmer of life, we began to wonder if we were the only people in this God-forsaken town.

Upon returning to the hotel, we entered the lounge, which contained a hardwood bar, stained-glass windows and an old-fashioned pool table. As we settled in to begin cooking our dinner in the common kitchen, one of the owner's cats became animated. We knew it couldn't be the smell of asparagus and potatoes we purchased from a roadside stand, so we dismissed its actions as another idiosyncrasy of The Blackball. Probably no mice.

But out of the darkness came the source of the cat's intent: a black bird, which probably had fallen down the chimney, flew through the room and crashed into the far window. Cyd and I recovered enough to move carefully in its direction only to have the bird make a bee-line right at us. We dodged. The cat leaped. The bird crashed, this time into a side window.

Not sure what we should do, I tried keeping the cat at bay while Cyd scouted the kitchen for a cloth or towel to capture the bird. Meanwhile, the bird was busy bouncing off walls and windows, followed closely by me and then the cat. Our break came when the bird fluttered to the floor near a fire exit. My heart pounded more frantically than prior to bungy-jumping as I neared the bird and the exit. I felt that with one lunge and swoop I could usher the bird to safety, but then I thought, what about the alarm? With the grace of a shortstop fielding a grounder and shoveling the ball to second, I opened the door and sent the bird on its way. No alarm bells. No embarrassing explanation. Just me, Cyd and the cat, which returned disappointed to its place near the fire.

We finished our meal and, before retiring to our room that night, listened to Big Band music on the juke box with the proprietor in the billiard room while he drank, discussed politics and told us of his days as a vice president of a company in Aukland. It was reassuring to see a man who had made a similar decision to ours, enjoying his life because he elected to change things. It didn't matter that in a few shorts weeks we would be home again; we were sure we'd made the right choice.

A WHALE OF A TIME IN KAIKOURA

Because the South Island is so narrow, we decided to cross back over to the east coast and spend a day or two in the fishing village of Kaikoura, renowned for its deep channels which are home to whales, great sharks and giant squid, some said to be as big as a bus. Upon arriving at the shore, the sun glistened off the snowcapped peaks of the Seaward and Inland Ranges as we drove the solitary road along the beach and into town. The hostel was "full up," so we made arrangements to stay with a young woman who rented out rooms above her house.

Another day brought clouds and the threat of rain, but we joined a handful of others crammed into a rescue speedboat that for the next hour would take us in search of whales and dolphins that feed in the rich currents off shore. A Maori man revved the engine and we were off, skipping across the breakers like the stones Cyd and I had tossed at the green pools. Prior to taking off, the crew had uttered a warning for anyone with a bad back or neck to speak up, and judging from the pounding we took it would have been a good idea for anybody seeing a chiropractor to stay behind.

The jostling blitz out to sea was well worth it when we saw the first black tail rising out of the water like a misplanted tree, flicking for a second as if waving good-bye, then silently dipping below the surface. It was in that first moment of awe that our guides pointed to the whale's "footprint," an oily, smooth outline in the water, which some experts believe is caused by the displaced mass as the 60-foot creature dives. This was only the first of a dozen whales we'd see on the overcast but uplifting day as we jetted from one sighting to the next, sidling up close to the beasts with the motor off and occasionally getting sprayed with water from the whale's spout.

The second part of the morning "cruise" took us south toward a rocky island and seal colony, whose inhabitants slept among the kelp and crevices protecting them from predators and making them difficult to see. After pointing out some rare Hectors Dolphins that played in the crashing surf, the guides promised us one more stop among a school of Dusky Dolphins that frequented the aqua-blue shoreline.

It wasn't long before we spotted our first dolphin, which flipped acrobatically out of the water as if it had been trained to do so on cue. More and more gray dolphins surrounded our boat, playing in its wake and snatching fish right before our eyes. We observed hundreds of bobbing fins like children eyeing a Christmas catalogue, while the guides told us about their increasing numbers and integral role in the food chain.

Later, in the invigorating chill of evening, still somewhat wobbly from the speedboat and day's excitement, Cyd and I took a brisk stroll around the untamed Kaikoura peninsula. Seals raised their heads from leeward rocks, keeping an eye on us as we kept our distance and maintained a non-threatening posture. As I looked out at the colony silhouetted against the white froth of the breakers, Cyd squeaked and grabbed me by the arm, almost causing me to jump right on top of the dead seal she had discovered. The decaying carcass, which had washed ashore, had a large bite taken out of it, which I immediately attributed to a shark attack. As we continued over the exposed rocks at low tide, we discussed how we might push the dead seal back into the sea. Immersed in conversation we walked right up on a large seal napping in a rock alcove. From a few feet away the 300-pound cow slowly raised her pointed brown head, flashed a set of sharp, ivory white teeth, and with a threatening bark sent us quickly on our way.

Neither Cyd or I will ever forget looking in the seal's eyes, threatening, yet forgiving, as we walked away. It was if we were being eyed with respect for not intruding on the animal's turf. Maybe it was our imagination, but now the seals along the exposed shoreline were less concerned with us too. The fear and anxiety that they exhibited upon our arrival seemed to have dissipated with that single bark.

The following day the weather's interminable game of cat-and-mouse continued. As if streaming through a giant magnifying glass, the sun bore down on us through the depleted ozone which is notorious for causing skin cancer in New Zealand and Australia. We made it to Picton in plenty of time for the ferry and enjoyed a clear day of sailing across the channel without even a hint of whitecaps, only a solitary seal that crossed our wake as if to say good-bye.

We took advantage of the good weather and pushed north and west toward Cape Taranaki, which we bypassed on our previous sprint to Wellington nearly a month ago. There, we hiked around Mt. Egmont, one of the most perfectly conical volcanoes in the world, and which from a distance on clear days appears to be floating in the Taranaki Bight off shore.

Our days in New Zealand were numbered and we cut back across the North Island hoping finally to get a chance to scale Tongariro's peaks, but the weather failed to cooperate again. A blizzard struck from out of nowhere, stranding a German hiker on the pass, necessitating his rescue. Pressed for time and certain the weather was just not going to cooperate on this trip, we opted instead to visit the healing thermal pools of Rotarua.

On the recommendation of Jacqui and Stella, whom we met on our initial ferry crossing, we chose to make the northern tip of New Zealand's Coromandel Peninsula our last stop before returning to the States, a sad and fast-approaching prospect that neither Cyd or I relished. Our final days at Tui Lodge were quiet and introspective, interrupted only by walks in the mud flats and a rigorous climb up Castle Rock, which revealed the odd combination of nearby timberlands and the Bay of Islands north of Aukland.

We spent our last full day in New Zealand recuperating from the long hike the day before through heavy brush and soggy trails. As we readied ourselves physically and mentally to return home, Cyd got a stylish haircut and convinced me to get another buzz cut, which I did in between washing and drying loads of laundry. As we left Coromandel and headed for Aukland, the rain returned to bid adieu, accompanying us the entire way to the airport.

Resigned to the fact that we were going home, we were somewhat disappointed that our flight was delayed due to mechanical problems. We would have to wait six hours for the connecting flight from Brisbane, then we could continue on the remaining segment to Honolulu.

From our booth in the airport pub, I saw Nigel's familiar face appear from behind a partition. He, too, was frustrated by the delay and scanning the area for a place to sit and drink. We flagged him down.

For hours we recounted stories from our separate but similar journeys in the constant rain of New Zealand. Nigel commented how he was looking forward to sunshine in Hawaii; we weren't as thrilled.

During our conversation we were interrupted by several other backpackers we had met in our travels over the previous six months who added to our menagerie of remembrances, mentioned their next destination and went on their way. I had devoted an entire journal section to names and addresses of people we met and promised that upon returning home I would contact each and every one.

The luster of traveling was fading in the waning minutes of our approaching departure time. I wanted to stay in New Zealand or go back in the direction we came, but at the same time I was ready for a break from cold showers and spicy food and bedding down in my sleeping bag in strange places. Nigel snapped me from my daydream dilemma with a short punch to the arm, followed by a verbal jab about my erroneous claim that it was only four hours to Hawaii: The flight would take more than eight hours before we touched down on US soil.

ALOHA ALSO MEANS GOOD-BYE

The customs agent's curt behavior upon arriving in Hawaii was rivaled only by the most difficult people we met on the trip, including the Chinese ticket-taker in Penang. They harassed Nigel about money, working in the US and not overstaying his visa, while questioning Cyd and I as if we were from a hostile country. No leis. No alohas. Just a straightforward "Passport, please."

We joined a crowd of tourists assembled outside for the bus to Honolulu.   There, a large, black attendant was chastising several Japanese tourists who took it upon themselves to form their own lines. "What! Do we have three lines here?" the attendant said. Cyd and I grinned from ear to ear at the familiar New York accent. We were welcomed home by his sarcastic jolt, and Nigel took care not to laugh until we did. After exchanging addresses and giving him a few pointers on the art of tipping, we said good-bye, not fully convinced it was for the last time.

It was Thanksgiving Day all over again as we had gained a reprieve by crossing the International Dateline. Cyd spent the day browsing through storefronts filled with Christmas decorations, while I visited a seaside park where Hawaiians picnicked in the hot sun. We met later for an old-fashioned turkey dinner at Denny's, complete with all the pumpkin pie we could eat for dessert. Having lost more than 15 pounds each, neither of us complained at the cook's generosity. In fact, we enjoyed yet another turkey feast the next day at Studebakers' Friday-night Thanksgiving party where, for the price of two beers, we gorged ourselves on turkey, yams, cranberry sauce and apple and pumpkin pie until we were sick. It felt good to be back in the land of plenty.

Making the most of an inter-island plane ticket and car-and-hotel package, over the next few days we flew to the other islands, trying to feel the fascination tourists showed and failing miserably in light of our extensive travels. Cyd commented that had we not just spent months in exotic, foreign places, we would be enjoying Hawaii immensely.

So, as we had for the past half year, we sought Hawaii's hidden treasures off the tourist track instead of reveling in the traditional promises all the travel brochures made. This was when our trip in Hawaii took a turn for the better, becoming yet another memorable travel jewel in our crown. One day we waded in the magical seven pools of Maui's eastern shore, the next we spent sunning on the desolate black sand beaches of the Big Island. Yet our most memorable and melancholy experience came as we hiked the silver sword trail winding through Haleakala Crater, a reminder of ethereal places we had encountered abroad.

The 12-hour trek through the bowels of Haleakala was more than we could have imagined even for this chain of islands where tourism long ago replaced agriculture as the chief form of income. We parked our car at 7,000 feet and hitched a ride to the peak with two rangers who approved of our hiking plans for the day and even more so of the details of our trip.

It was as cool and windy as one might expect atop a 15,000-foot peak, but the cloudless sky let the warming sun pour in. After a few minutes surveying the city-size bowl of the crater, we began our descent, which would bring us out near the top of the clouds bunched around the lower rim. The various hues of gravel made me think of the moon surface and we found it difficult to traverse the steep, eroded switchbacks. Silver swords, spiny plants resembling sea anemones, which had almost disappeared from the crater, marked the path on the way down.

Several hours of leisurely hiking took us through lunar landscapes and rolling hills of hardened lava into the outback of the crater. Cyd had developed shin splints and we slowed our pace, which allowed for even greater inspection of the surroundings. Nearing the end of the trail, we walked through a rainbow and met the first person we'd seen during the day. He was a real estate salesman on a short evening jog into the crater basin, who took a few minutes to catch his breath, assess our experiences in Hawaii, and leave his business card before going on his way. Things that had bothered us about the United States in the past now seemed amusing and we laughed that he'd found a way to make his pitch in the most isolated spot on the island.

The pain in Cyd's knees was getting worse, so I shouldered her weight as we climbed the great stone path rising 1,000 feet from the base to the parking lot and our car. Emerging from the brush and cacti, we came face-to-face with Old Sol, resting atop the clouds in a warm orange glow of sunset. It was just another of the rebirths we had experienced along the way. What one local had promised would be a religious experience certainly was, and we felt revitalized. We drove down the hill through the clouds and into darkness, aiming the car for the distant lights of town that now mirrored the twinkling stars above.

AROUND THE WORLD IN 180 DAYS

It was with regret and an equal amount of relief that we caught the red-eye to Los Angeles, where we planned to stay with Cyd's friends for a few days while reorienting ourselves to the States. Assimilating to US lifestyle didn't take long as we attended a Lakers' game, ate dinner at Jack-in-the-Box, toured one of the world's largest malls and then drove the freeway to visit Cyd's aunt and uncle in San Diego. Our last welcoming came at the airline check-in counter at LAX, where the coifed woman insisted politely that I would have to put my backpack into a plastic bag to ensure nothing got lost. I told her that we had just traveled more than 40,000 miles without losing a thing or ever once putting our backpacks in plastic, but she insisted.

Anxiety clutched at our chests as we rose from LAX into the clear skies above California. It was good to be back in the United States, flying over the snow-splattered Painted Desert toward Tampa and the first of many family reunions. We had started the trip railing about everything that was wrong with our country and complaining that we had to return to the mess, but now, back near the street lights and shopping malls, amid throngs of well-fed and educated people, within reach of healthy food and water

172

and sanitation, among family and friends we forgot all that was wrong with America.

My brother met us at the Tampa baggage terminal where, for some unexplainable reason, I wasn't able to find my backpack. After all, hadn't the woman at LAX placed it in the plastic bag ensuring safety of all its contents? I would later discover it was separated from its bag and rerouted to Miami. It was almost as if I could hear the gate attendant whispering, "Welcome home."

The days ahead included visits with my family in Florida and stops at Cyd's relatives in North Carolina. In each case, we recounted tales of adventure late into the night as we opened parcels we had shipped from Bali and Singapore. We revisited many places from the trip through the sights and smells unleashed by opening yet another carton of gifts, this one from Bangkok. Finally, we got a ride from Cyd's grandparents to the Charlotte airport, where we boarded the last flight for home.

My younger sister, who kept Cyd's car while we were gone, met us at the Pittsburgh airport terminal along with her family. We returned to their house where my grandmother greeted us as if we were beings from another planet. "You're so beautiful. You're so beautiful," she kept repeating, hugging us tight so we'd never leave again.

As we recounted our stories yet another time, as we would again and again over the next few months, I thought how difficult it was for everyone to grasp what we were talking about, especially Grams. She smiled the same polite smile that Mo and Hari had displayed when we tried to describe where the United States was in relation to Lombok by drawing a map in the sand, but to her all that mattered was that we were home. And that was good enough for me.

We unveiled yet another cache of gifts, which this time included sarongs and wool slippers, foreign currencies and Thai toys. When my sister hollered at me and my nephew for shooting darts from an Indonesian blow-gun into the kitchen door, I knew for certain we were home.

That night we revved up Cyd's car and nervously drove the familiar, memory-filled streets of Pittsburgh. Possibly delaying the inevitable return home, we went past Cyd's house and drove an additional two hours to Erie, where we traded more hugs and kisses and gifts, this time with Cyd's family. Over the next few days, Cyd's mom prepared various feasts and we all took turns playing the carved mahogany flute which resembled a grade-school recorder with the weird head of an Indonesian idol as its mouthpiece. Christmas came and went quickly in a wave of gluttony and we apprehensively waved good-bye on our way home for the last time.

All of the arcs we had penned on our maps more than a year ago were now complete. We faced the prospect of waking from our dream and beginning the rat race all over again, which we hoped we might somehow be able to slow down and manage better than before.

Exactly six months to the day after we first left the country, we sat in the quiet darkness of Cyd's living room, sleepily awaiting the New Year's fireworks which would sparkle at The Point, the rumble and boom eventually echoing its way to us seconds later, reminding us of glaciers calving and the thunder of monsoons. For weeks prior to our arrival we had planned on surprising our friends at a late-night party, but we chose instead to relax and remember the faces and places we'd seen over the past months, trying not to think about what lay ahead.

Sleep came peacefully with the realization we had met friendly, unforgettable people and sampled other-worldly foods and cultures by simply following our noses in an easterly direction, happening on sites and taking mental photographs we would appreciate for the rest of our lives. Living a dream in the manner of Messieurs Fogg and Passepartout, we had encountered Indians and elephants and pitfalls of our own, and much like that famous duo from Jules Verne's classic, we had discovered our biggest challenge was not weather or language or tide, but time.

174

Epilogue

It has been four years since we came home from our trip, and we are still reaping rewards from having done it. I am writing and pursuing a Master's degree in counseling, and Cyd has fulfilled her dream of becoming a teacher. We continue to travel regularly and at length, having purposely chosen careers which would allow us to do so. Subsequent trips have taken us to Greece, Alaska, Egypt and Central America, site of our honeymoon. And now we are about to embark on an adventure of another kind, the birth of our first child, Ana, who will travel with us to the Olympics before her first birthday.

Since coming home the question we've been asked most often about our trip is "How did we do it?" The answer is, "We just did." Embarking on a trip of this magnitude, literally going around the world in 180 days, didn't require guts or genius or a whole lot of money. All it took was planning and fortitude to shove off and never look back. It was kind of like diving into an ice-cold swimming pool: shocking and refreshing at the same time.

Yet, taking a chance like this was not a great risk either. In fact, when considering that unlike most of the people we met along the way, we would be returning to the most bountiful country in the world, it wasn't risky at all. People from other countries do it every day. Many are Europeans on vacation or college break or simply sorting out what to do with their lives. Others, mostly Australians and Canadians, take time out from the sometimes frenetic pace of their work-a-day worlds. Still others from island nations such as England, Japan and New Zealand are searching for foreign cultures and natural wonder outside their own little worlds.

Though we shared few physical boundaries with most of the other travelers we met, we all had one thing in common: the desire to see the rest of the world through other people's eyes. Almost to the person, we chose to temporarily cast off our fortunate lot in life and take a back seat to the fate and whimsy of other cultures and societies. In our hearts we hoped that somehow the friendships we made, the time and money we spent, the words we

175

exchanged, would mean as much to the people we met as it did to us.

As part of our personal odyssey we left behind our egocentric mind-set and took a walk on the simple side. Living abroad was difficult and not always fun. We eagerly traded hardships for opportunities to eat strange food, speak tongue-twisting languages and experience first-hand other people's joys and sorrows. And as every country changed in size, topography, government and tradition, we tried to conform to the mores and customs that made each place and the people who lived there unique.

We didn't always triumph in our quest to live like the people of various colors and creeds and cultures along our route. That would have been impossible. Yet once back among our friends and family, we knew that no matter how sick or frustrated or unfortunate we were while on the trip, it had been a positive, life-changing experience.

If you, too, are interested in seeing the world as others see it, I say, just do it. You'll find the education and experiences of travel will far outweigh any time, energy and money you'll invest. In fact, living abroad for a period of time amongst different peoples and cultures, in some of the most peaceful and majestic settings in the world, is less expensive than daily existence in the US.

All you have to do is close your eyes, put your finger on the globe and give it a whirl.

Tony Del Prete has traveled on six continents and written about his experiences for travel magazines, trade journals and newspapers. He has also co-authored, edited and ghost-written various self-help and best-selling business books. He, his wife and daughter live in Pittsburgh, Pennsylvania.